MathFlare

Name: _______________________

Class: ___________

Teacher: _______________________

Introduction

As parents and educators, we recognize the pivotal role mathematics plays in shaping a child's academic journey and future success. Yet, the path to mathematical proficiency can often seem daunting, fraught with challenges and complexities. That's where the transformative power of MathFlare Workbooks shine through, illuminating the way forward with clarity, precision, and purpose.

Introducing MathFlare Workbooks – a beacon of guidance, a testament to excellence, and a catalyst for achievement. Crafted with meticulous care and expertise, MathFlare Workbooks stand as paragons of educational excellence, designed to nurture young minds, ignite a passion for learning, and develop a deep-rooted understanding of mathematical concepts.

Picture this: your child eagerly delves into the pages of Mathflare Workbook, greeted by a step-by-step guide illuminated with vivid examples that demystify complex mathematical concepts. With each turn of the page, they embark on a journey of discovery, encountering thoughtfully curated practice questions that reinforce learning and hone problem-solving skills. And when they unveil the answers to those very questions, a sense of accomplishment blossoms within them – a tangible reward for their hard work and dedication.

But MathFlare Workbooks are more than just tools for learning; they are pathways to comprehension, fostering a deep-seated understanding of mathematical concepts through a sequential, logical flow. From fundamental principles to advanced problem-solving strategies, every chapter builds upon the last, ensuring a robust foundation upon which future knowledge can be constructed.

As parents, we yearn for nothing more than to see our children thrive, to witness the spark of inspiration ignited within them as they conquer academic challenges with confidence and poise. MathFlare Workbooks serve as partners in this noble endeavor, offering not just practice questions, but the keys to unlocking a world of opportunity.

And for teachers, MathFlare Workbooks stand as invaluable allies in the quest to cultivate mathematical proficiency in the classroom. With answers readily available, instructors can focus on guiding and nurturing their students, confident in the knowledge that MathFlare Workbooks provide a solid framework upon which to build.

In the pages of MathFlare Workbooks, we find not just the promise of academic excellence, but the seeds of a brighter tomorrow. So let us embrace the power of mathematics, let us champion the journey of learning, and let us pave the way for a generation of young minds poised to shape the world. With MathFlare Workbooks as our guide, the possibilities are infinite, and the future, bright.

Table of Contents

MathFlare
2
MATH WORKBOOK
Addition Subtraction
Multiplication
Place Value and Expanded Notations
Geometry
Step by Step Guide and Essential Practice with Answers
MathFlare Publishing

MathFlare
2-3
MATH WORKBOOK
Addition Subtraction
Multiplication and Division
Place Value and Expanded Notations
Geometry
Step by Step Guide and Essential Practice with Answers
MathFlare Publishing

MathFlare
3
MATH WORKBOOK
Multiplication and Division
Decimals
Place Value and Expanded Notations
Fractions and Geometry
Step by Step Guide and Essential Practice with Answers
MathFlare Publishing

MathFlare
1
MATH WORKBOOK
Counting and Numbers
Addition and Subtraction
Place Value and Expanded Notations
Understanding Time
Step by Step Guide and Essential Practice with Answers
MathFlare Publishing

MathFlare
1-2
MATH WORKBOOK
Counting and Numbers
Addition and Subtraction
Place Value and Expanded Notations
Understanding Time
Step by Step Guide and Essential Practice with Answers
MathFlare Publishing

MathFlare
3-4
MATH WORKBOOK
Addition Subtraction
Multiplication Division
Place Value and Expanded Notations
Fractions and Geometry
Step by Step Guide and Essential Practice with Answers
MathFlare Publishing

MathFlare
4
MATH WORKBOOK
Addition Subtraction
Multiplication Division
Place Value and Expanded Notations
Fractions and Geometry
Step by Step Guide and Essential Practice with Answers
MathFlare Publishing

MathFlare
4-5
MATH WORKBOOK
Multiplication Division
Place Value and Expanded Notations
Fractions and Geometry
Unit Conversion
Step by Step Guide and Essential Practice with Answers
MathFlare Publishing

MathFlare
Grade 5
MATH WORKBOOK
Step by Step Guide and Essential Practice with Answers
Multiplication Division
Place Value and Expanded Notations
Fractions and Geometry
Unit Conversion
MathFlare Publishing

MathFlare
Grade 5-6
MATH WORKBOOK
Step by Step Guide and Essential Practice with Answers
Multiplication Division
Place Value and Expanded Notations
Fractions and Geometry
Units and Statistics
MathFlare Publishing

MathFlare
Grade 6
MATH WORKBOOK
Step by Step Guide and Essential Practice with Answers
Integers and Statistics
Arithmetic and Pre-Algebra
Fractions and Geometry
Ratio and Percentage
MathFlare Publishing

MathFlare
Grade 6-7
MATH WORKBOOK
Step by Step Guide and Essential Practice with Answers
Arithmetic and Pre-Algebra
Ratio, Percent Proportion
Geometry
Statistics
MathFlare Publishing

MathFlare
Grade 7
MATH WORKBOOK
Step by Step Guide and Essential Practice with Answers
Pre-Algebra
Ratio, Percent Proportion
Geometry
Statistics
MathFlare Publishing

MathFlare
Grade 7-8
MATH WORKBOOK
Step by Step Guide and Essential Practice with Answers
Pre-Algebra
Ratio, Percent Proportion
Geometry and Cartesian Plane
Statistics
MathFlare Publishing

MathFlare
Grade 8-9
MATH WORKBOOK
Step by Step Guide and Essential Practice with Answers
Pre-Algebra
Ratio, Proportion and Percentage
Linear Equations
Geometry and Cartesian Plane
MathFlare Publishing

MathFlare
Grade 8
MATH WORKBOOK
Step by Step Guide and Essential Practice with Answers
Pre-Algebra
Percentage
Linear Equations
Geometry
MathFlare Publishing

Addition and Subtraction

Addition with Regrouping

When we do addition, we combine numbers. But sometimes, when we're adding numbers, we might need to regroup. Regrouping means we must move a number from one place to another, usually to the next column, to get the right answer.

For Example: Let's take an example of adding 33 and 79 together:

$$\begin{array}{r} 33 \\ +\ \underline{79} \end{array}$$

First, we start by adding the digits in the ones place: 3 + 9 = 12. We write down the 2 in the ones place and carry over the 1 to the tens place.

$$\begin{array}{r} 1 \\ 33 \\ +\ \underline{79} \\ 2 \end{array}$$

Now, we add the digits in the tens place, along with the carry-over: 3 + 7 + 1 = 11. We write down the 1 in the tens place and carry over the 1 to the hundreds place.

$$\begin{array}{r} 1 \\ 22 \\ +\ \underline{89} \\ 111 \end{array}$$

This process of carrying over helps us accurately add numbers, especially when they're larger.

Subtraction with Regrouping

Subtraction is a key math operation where we find the difference between two numbers. Sometimes, when we subtract, we might need to regroup, which means borrowing from the next column.

Let's take an example of subtracting 36 from 63:

First, we start by subtracting the digits in the ones place: 3 - 6. Since 3 is less than 6, we need to regroup. We borrow 1 from the tens place, making it 5 tens instead of 6, and add it to the ones place.

So, 3 becomes 13, and then we subtract 6.

$$
\begin{array}{r}
6\ 13 \\
-\ 3\ 6 \\
\hline
7
\end{array}
$$

Now, we subtract the tens place digits: 5 - 3 = 2

$$
\begin{array}{r}
5 \\
\cancel{6}\ 13 \\
-\ 3\ 6 \\
\hline
2\ 7
\end{array}
$$

This process of regrouping or borrowing helps us accurately subtract numbers, especially when the top digit is smaller than the bottom one.

Let's solve problems from the exercises:

$$
\begin{array}{r}
99 \\
+\ 68 \\
\hline
167
\end{array}
\qquad
\begin{array}{r}
33 \\
-\ 28 \\
\hline
5
\end{array}
$$

Addition and Subtraction: Unknown Numbers

When we have a situation where we need to find the missing number in an equation, we're usually solving for an unknown.

In this case, we have the equation $20 - \_\_\_ = 12$.

We're trying to figure out what number we need to subtract from 20 to get 12.

We know that $20 - \_\_\_ = 12$, so we can subtract 12 from 20:

$$20 - 12 = 8$$

Let's solve problems from exercises:

$$63 + \underline{\ 37\ } = 100$$

$$25 - \underline{\ 20\ } = 5$$

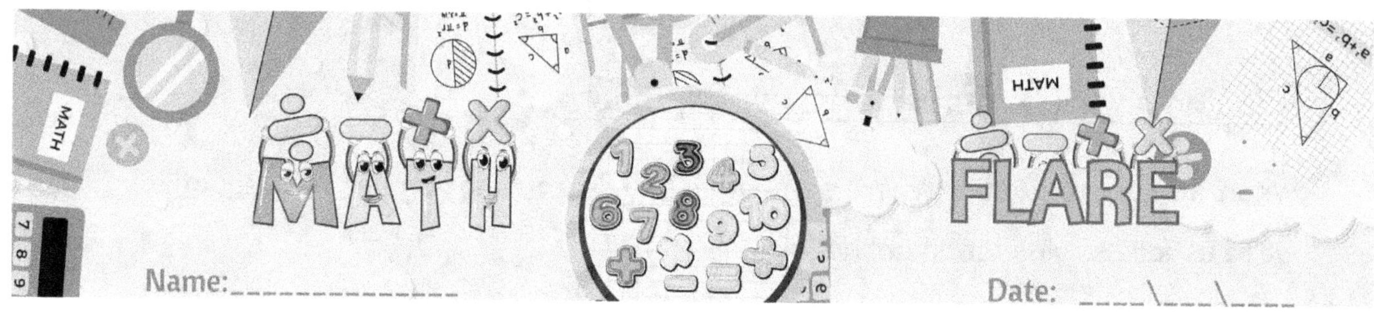

Addition: 1 through 20

Find the Sum.

1.   14
   + 1

2.   12
   + 13

3.   10
   + 3

4.   13
   + 4

5.   4
   + 8

6.   4
   + 5

7.   3
   + 6

8.   8
   + 19

9.   6
   + 9

10.   3
   + 14

11.   14
   + 3

12.   14
   + 10

13.   3
   + 8

14.   16
   + 12

15.   15
   + 1

16.   20
   + 12

17.   17
   + 5

18.   4
   + 10

19.   8
   + 2

20.   13
   + 3

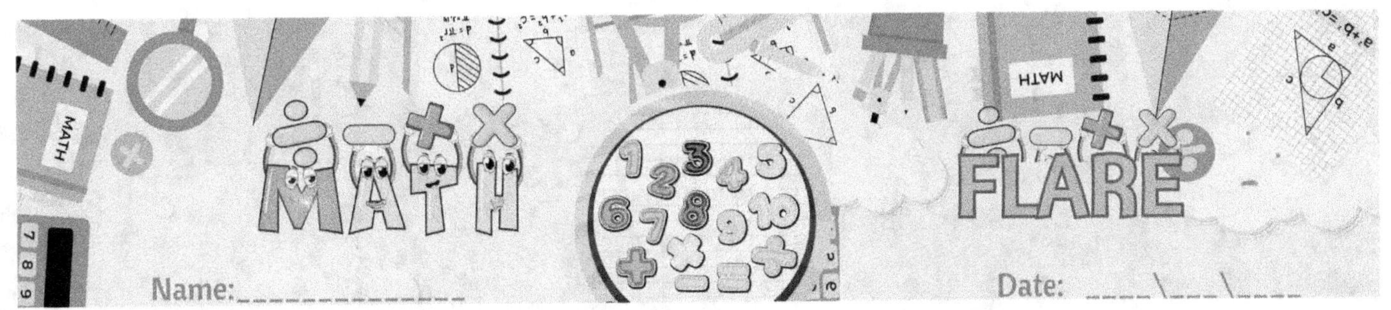

21. 20 + 8	22. 17 + 4	23. 14 + 9	24. 13 + 15	25. 3 + 18
26. 3 + 12	27. 7 + 3	28. 19 + 20	29. 19 + 6	30. 8 + 12
31. 12 + 4	32. 5 + 11	33. 10 + 4	34. 16 + 16	35. 2 + 1
36. 2 + 12	37. 3 + 4	38. 10 + 7	39. 13 + 19	40. 14 + 8

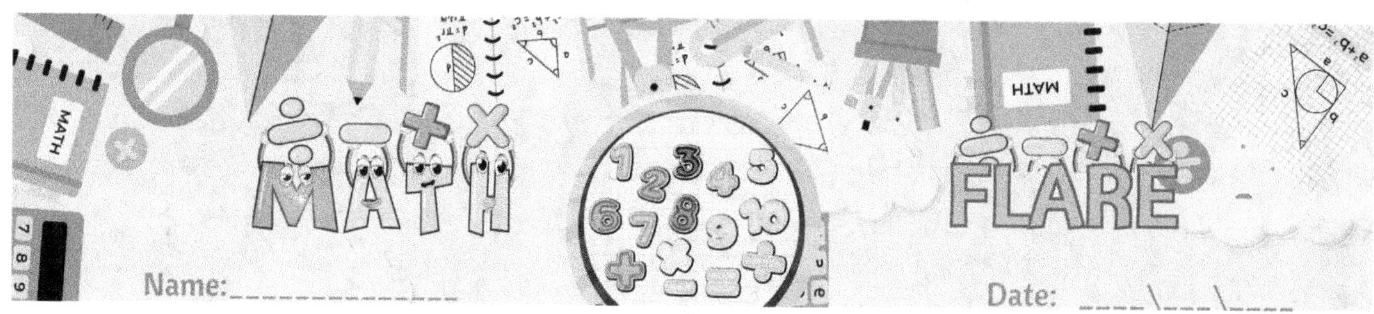

41. 19 + 1	42. 18 + 3	43. 10 + 5	44. 18 + 2	45. 11 + 9
46. 15 + 9	47. 20 + 16	48. 4 + 7	49. 14 + 11	50. 13 + 17
51. 15 + 3	52. 17 + 11	53. 13 + 13	54. 8 + 1	55. 13 + 20
56. 13 + 12	57. 6 + 3	58. 2 + 5	59. 6 + 15	60. 6 + 13

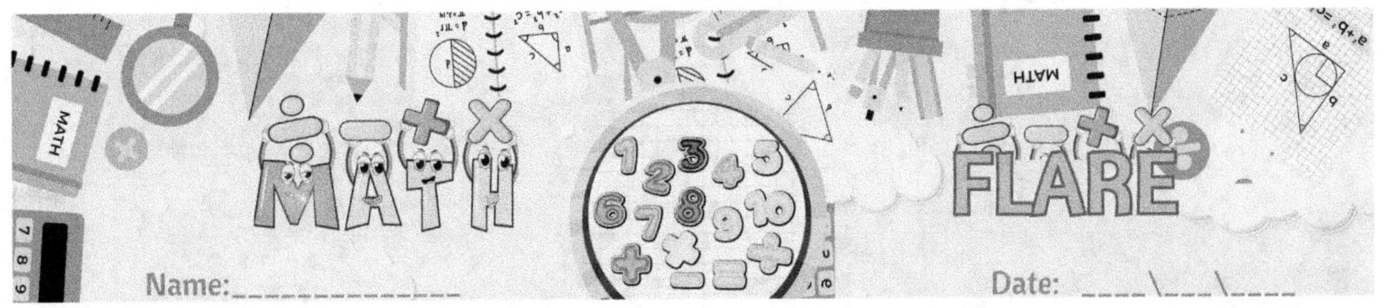

61. 18 + 15	62. 17 + 14	63. 4 + 14	64. 4 + 6	65. 7 + 16
66. 6 + 19	67. 15 + 14	68. 8 + 17	69. 2 + 3	70. 15 + 15
71. 16 + 9	72. 11 + 1	73. 6 + 10	74. 6 + 18	75. 12 + 3
76. 4 + 4	77. 14 + 16	78. 1 + 19	79. 10 + 2	80. 15 + 10

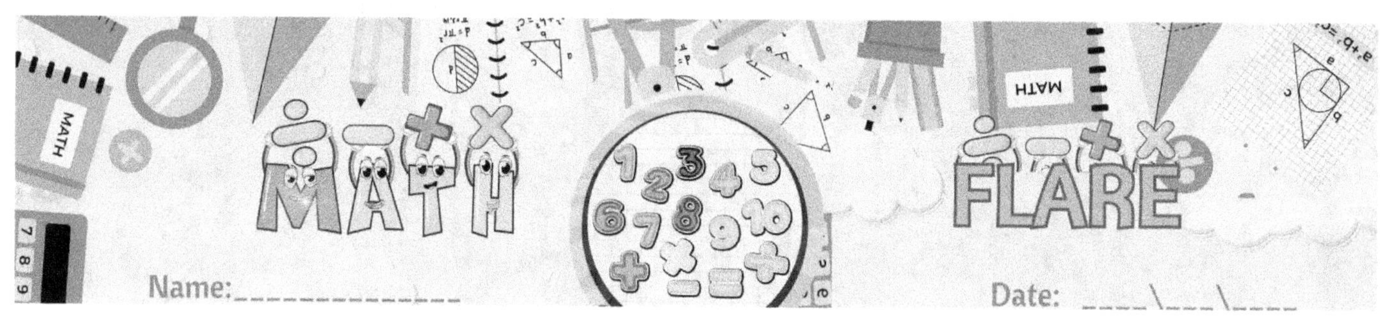

81. 6 + 11	82. 18 + 4	83. 10 + 12	84. 8 + 9	85. 12 + 17
86. 19 + 3	87. 1 + 16	88. 17 + 16	89. 11 + 5	90. 5 + 19
91. 8 + 20	92. 8 + 6	93. 3 + 3	94. 20 + 14	95. 11 + 4
96. 11 + 8	97. 4 + 13	98. 17 + 7	99. 2 + 19	100. 19 + 12

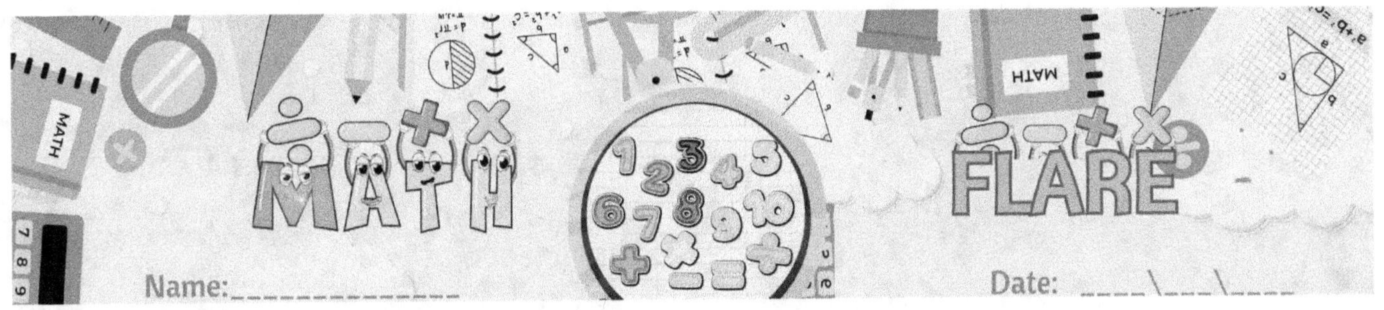

Addition: 1 through 20

Find the Sum.

101. $18 + 19 =$ _______________

102. $2 + 13 =$ _______________

103. $10 + 15 =$ _______________

104. $13 + 12 =$ _______________

105. $13 + 2 =$ _______________

106. $1 + 18 =$ _______________

107. $16 + 3 =$ _______________

108. $6 + 9 =$ _______________

109. $14 + 7 =$ _______________

110. $19 + 12 =$ _______________

111. $1 + 9 =$ _______________

112. $12 + 2 =$ _______________

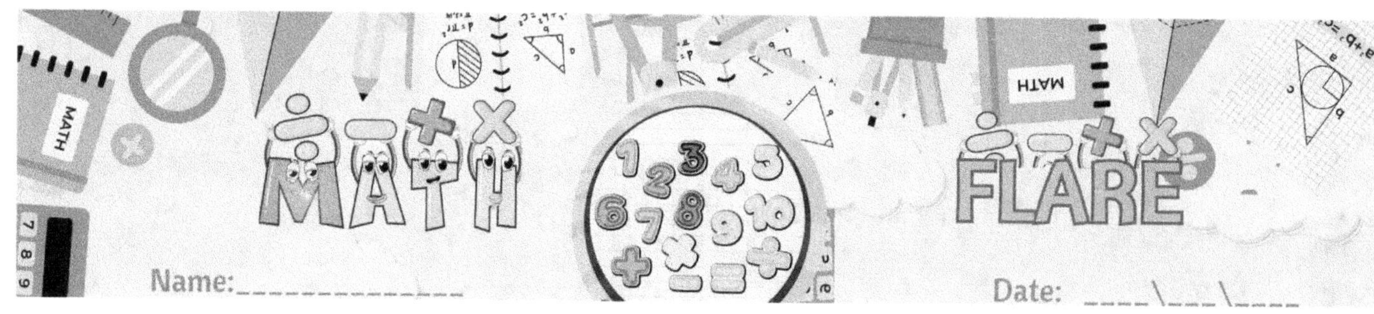

113. 19 + 9 = _______________

114. 12 + 1 = _______________

115. 7 + 2 = _______________

116. 6 + 8 = _______________

117. 5 + 9 = _______________

118. 17 + 13 = _______________

119. 3 + 18 = _______________

120. 18 + 9 = _______________

121. 1 + 7 = _______________

122. 13 + 16 = _______________

123. 7 + 4 = _______________

124. 4 + 11 = _______________

125. 5 + 12 = _______________

126. 9 + 11 = _______________

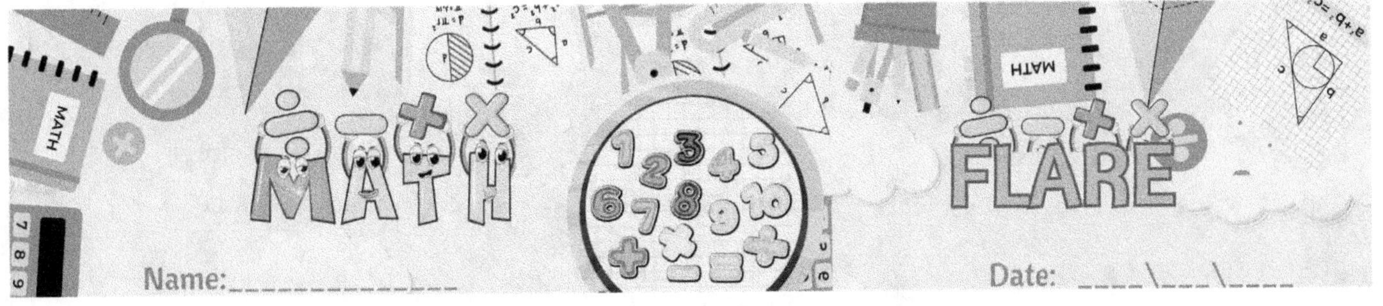

127. 17 + 7 = _______________

128. 11 + 10 = _______________

129. 7 + 1 = _______________

130. 14 + 2 = _______________

131. 4 + 13 = _______________

132. 6 + 12 = _______________

133. 15 + 14 = _______________

134. 14 + 8 = _______________

135. 7 + 13 = _______________

136. 7 + 16 = _______________

137. 12 + 14 = _______________

138. 16 + 16 = _______________

139. 15 + 16 = _______________

140. 6 + 2 = _______________

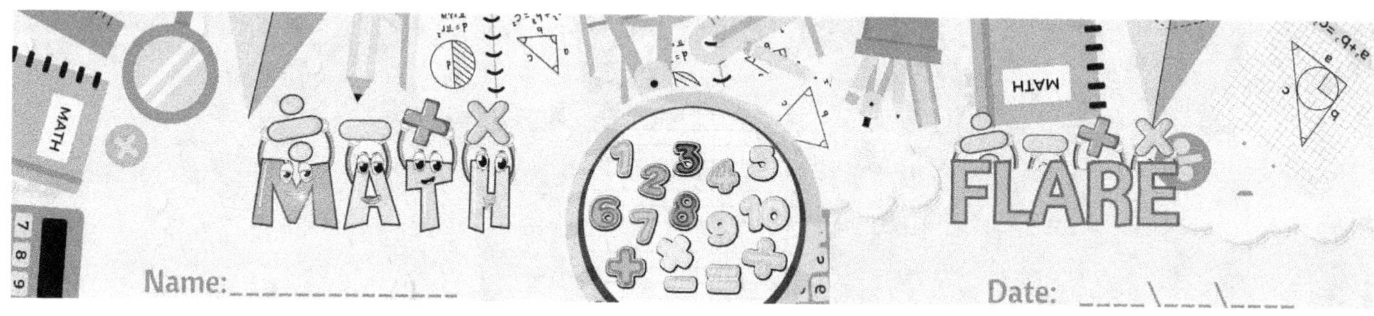

141. 16 + 15 = _______________

142. 11 + 17 = _______________

143. 18 + 8 = _______________

144. 7 + 3 = _______________

145. 5 + 17 = _______________

146. 2 + 2 = _______________

147. 9 + 15 = _______________

148. 6 + 13 = _______________

149. 3 + 7 = _______________

150. 15 + 18 = _______________

151. 14 + 11 = _______________

152. 6 + 18 = _______________

153. 16 + 11 = _______________

154. 19 + 20 = _______________

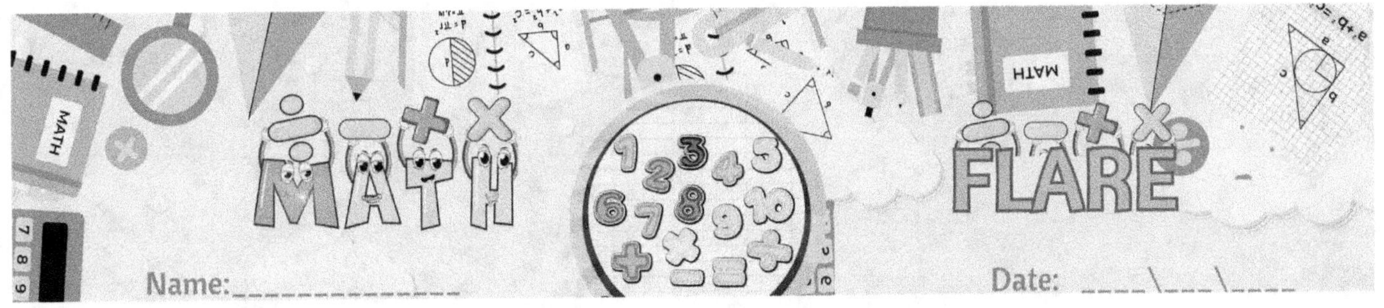

155. 4 + 17 = _______________

156. 11 + 19 = _______________

157. 7 + 5 = _______________

158. 11 + 12 = _______________

159. 6 + 5 = _______________

160. 7 + 11 = _______________

161. 17 + 6 = _______________

162. 10 + 20 = _______________

163. 14 + 5 = _______________

164. 3 + 1 = _______________

165. 16 + 7 = _______________

166. 3 + 4 = _______________

167. 12 + 11 = _______________

168. 3 + 2 = _______________

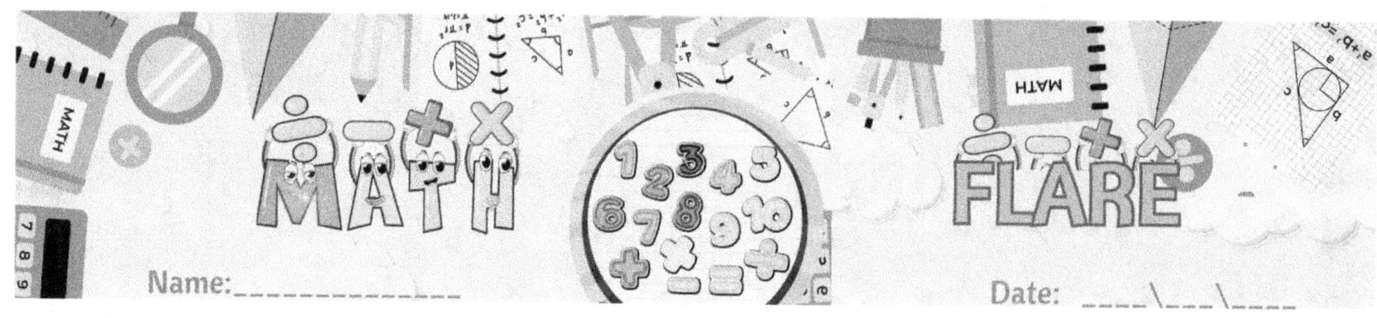

169. 10 + 12 = __________

170. 6 + 6 = __________

171. 5 + 2 = __________

172. 3 + 11 = __________

173. 6 + 1 = __________

174. 15 + 5 = __________

175. 12 + 5 = __________

176. 2 + 19 = __________

177. 7 + 19 = __________

178. 15 + 11 = __________

179. 9 + 5 = __________

180. 10 + 3 = __________

181. 13 + 14 = __________

182. 13 + 15 = __________

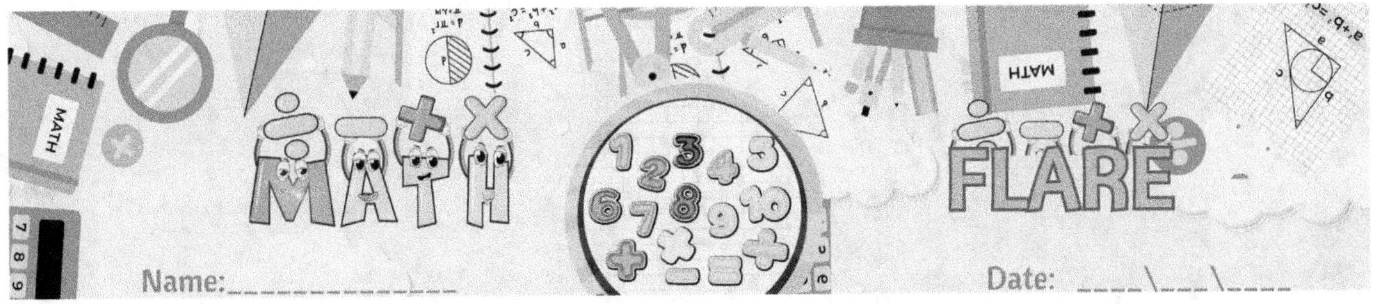

183. 18 + 3 = _______________

184. 3 + 12 = _______________

185. 15 + 13 = _______________

186. 2 + 12 = _______________

187. 15 + 17 = _______________

188. 18 + 1 = _______________

189. 18 + 15 = _______________

190. 19 + 14 = _______________

191. 13 + 17 = _______________

192. 2 + 1 = _______________

193. 19 + 5 = _______________

194. 8 + 2 = _______________

195. 12 + 18 = _______________

196. 19 + 15 = _______________

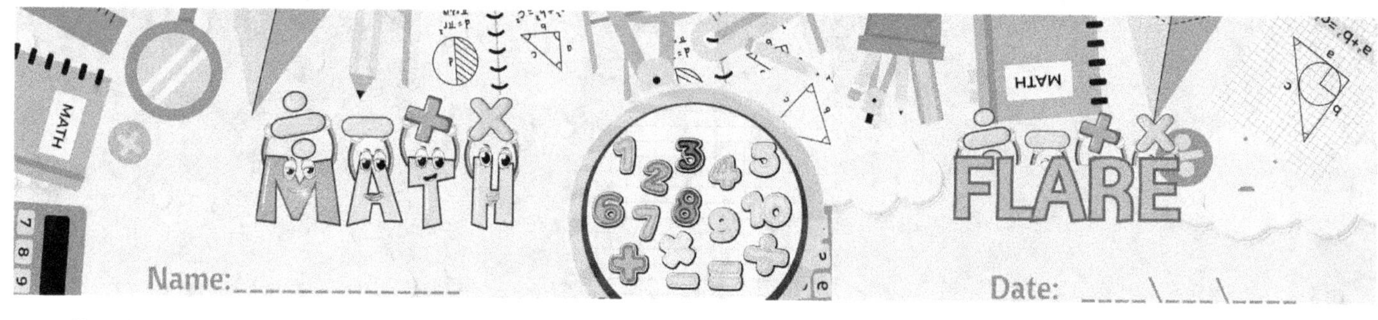

Subtraction: 1 through 20

Find the Difference.

197.	198.	199.	200.	201.
11 − 7	2 − 1	17 − 4	16 − 11	11 − 9

202.	203.	204.	205.	206.
5 − 3	12 − 6	19 − 3	17 − 10	13 − 5

207.	208.	209.	210.	211.
16 − 1	13 − 7	6 − 1	20 − 17	18 − 4

212.	213.	214.	215.	216.
10 − 9	2 − 2	13 − 10	19 − 6	4 − 3

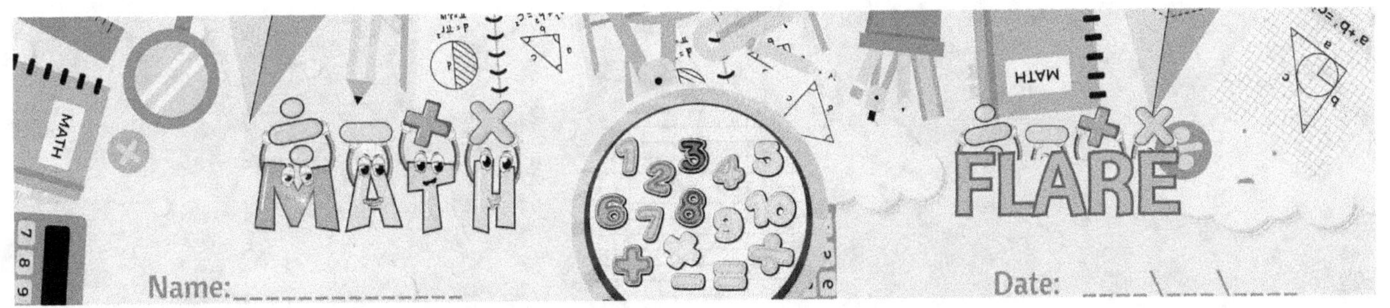

217. 8 − 4	218. 16 − 6	219. 13 − 12	220. 3 − 2	221. 3 − 1
222. 17 − 2	223. 3 − 3	224. 11 − 4	225. 9 − 5	226. 17 − 12
227. 15 − 2	228. 9 − 4	229. 10 − 2	230. 12 − 5	231. 5 − 1
232. 14 − 10	233. 7 − 3	234. 17 − 6	235. 18 − 9	236. 16 − 9

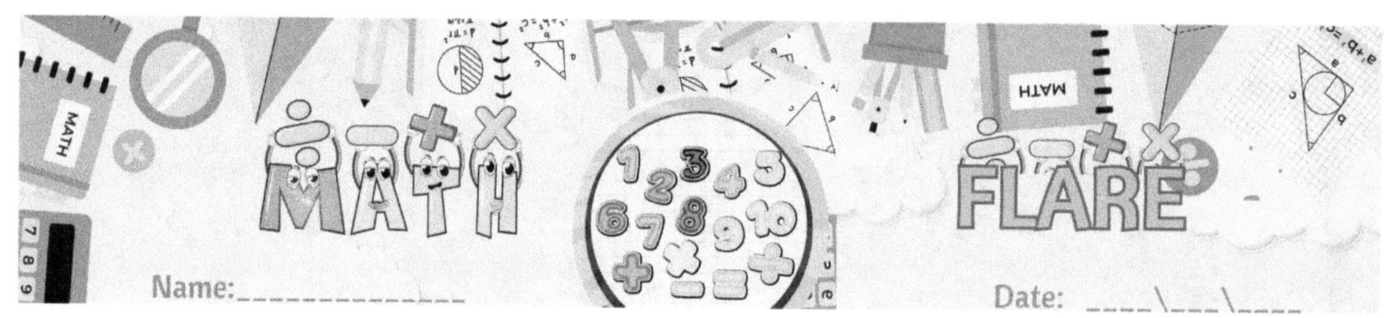

237. 5 − 4	238. 19 − 13	239. 14 − 11	240. 4 − 4	241. 10 − 7
242. 17 − 13	243. 20 − 16	244. 10 − 3	245. 9 − 2	246. 17 − 5
247. 1 − 1	248. 14 − 7	249. 18 − 11	250. 19 − 17	251. 11 − 6
252. 19 − 11	253. 14 − 5	254. 6 − 2	255. 13 − 1	256. 9 − 9

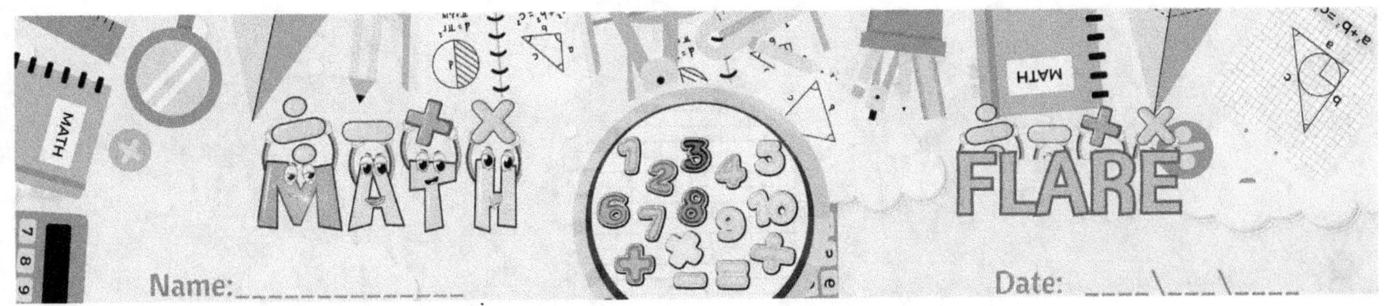

257. 6 − 5	258. 16 − 8	259. 15 − 5	260. 19 − 18	261. 15 − 6
262. 6 − 3	263. 18 − 17	264. 11 − 8	265. 13 − 6	266. 16 − 15
267. 10 − 6	268. 17 − 15	269. 8 − 1	270. 19 − 15	271. 19 − 14
272. 14 − 12	273. 19 − 2	274. 13 − 11	275. 6 − 6	276. 20 − 5

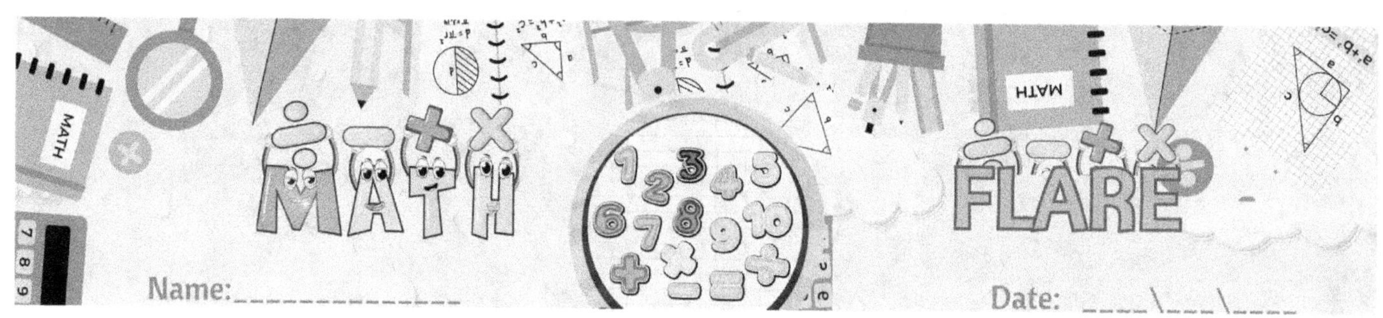

277.	278.	279.	280.	281.
18 − 10	8 − 6	20 − 19	12 − 10	15 − 14

282.	283.	284.	285.	286.
9 − 7	16 − 2	9 − 8	4 − 2	9 − 3

287.	288.	289.	290.	291.
19 − 4	19 − 12	5 − 2	10 − 5	18 − 6

292.	293.	294.	295.	296.
4 − 1	18 − 12	15 − 13	18 − 7	8 − 7

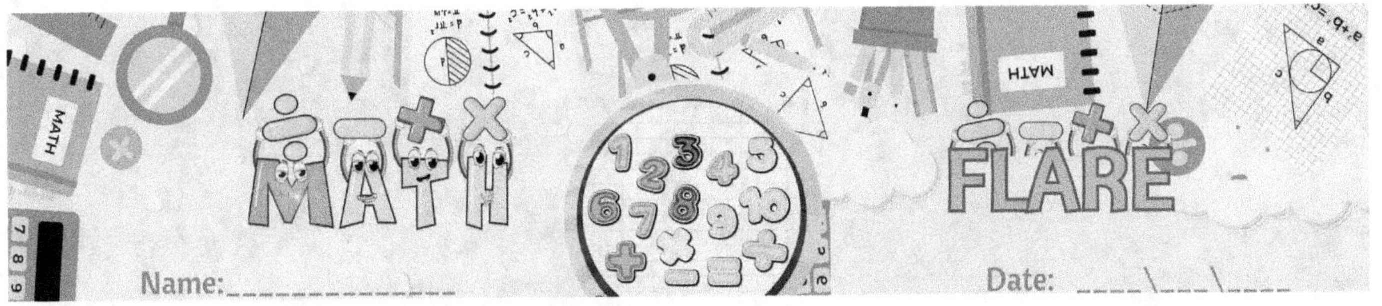

Subtraction: 1 through 20

Find the Difference.

297. 5 − 5 = _______________

298. 2 − 1 = _______________

299. 7 − 7 = _______________

300. 18 − 10 = _______________

301. 7 − 2 = _______________

302. 12 − 12 = _______________

303. 3 − 1 = _______________

304. 9 − 3 = _______________

305. 15 − 2 = _______________

306. 7 − 4 = _______________

307. 6 − 4 = _______________

308. 11 − 10 = _______________

309. 11 − 6 = _______________

310. 19 − 12 = _______________

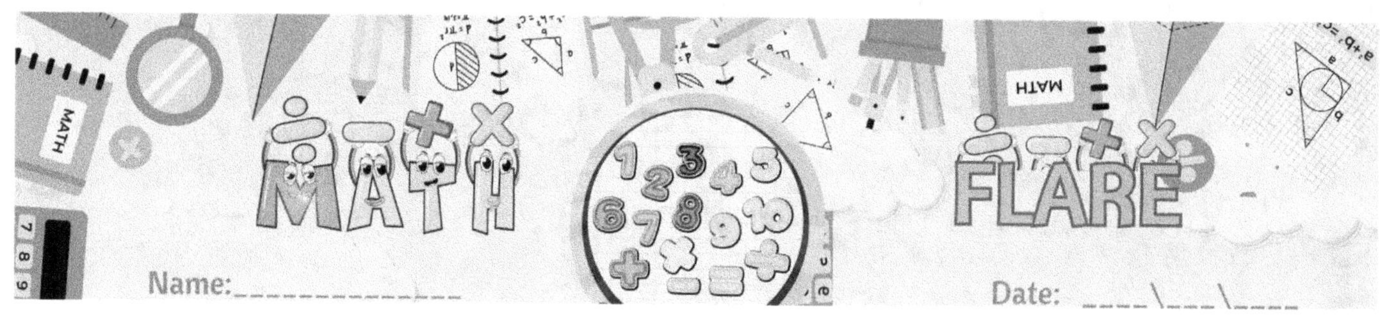

311. 13 - 6 = _______________

312. 19 - 4 = _______________

313. 6 - 3 = _______________

314. 12 - 9 = _______________

315. 16 - 13 = _______________

316. 2 - 2 = _______________

317. 12 - 4 = _______________

318. 19 - 7 = _______________

319. 11 - 8 = _______________

320. 16 - 1 = _______________

321. 4 - 3 = _______________

322. 9 - 1 = _______________

323. 15 - 5 = _______________

324. 4 - 4 = _______________

325. 14 - 5 = _______________

326. 16 - 16 = _______________

327. 5 - 2 = _______________

328. 9 - 5 = _______________

329. 17 - 13 = _______________

330. 17 - 16 = _______________

331. 18 - 4 = _______________

332. 16 - 10 = _______________

333. 6 - 2 = _______________

334. 15 - 4 = _______________

335. 11 - 9 = _______________

336. 13 - 3 = _______________

337. 18 - 6 = _______________

338. 3 - 2 = _______________

339. 11 - 7 = _______________

340. 12 - 8 = _______________

341. 18 - 13 = _______________

342. 5 - 1 = _______________

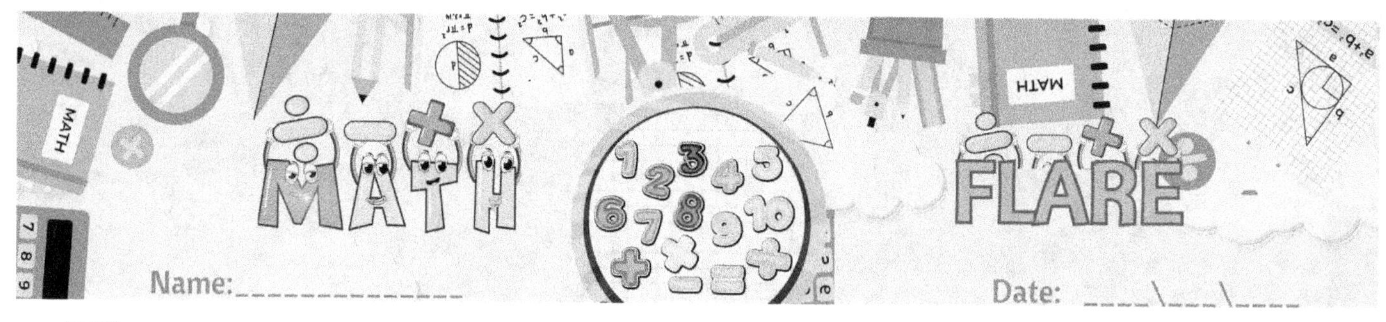

343. 19 - 11 = _______________

344. 19 - 15 = _______________

345. 9 - 8 = _______________

346. 1 - 1 = _______________

347. 17 - 10 = _______________

348. 14 - 11 = _______________

349. 20 - 4 = _______________

350. 19 - 2 = _______________

351. 3 - 3 = _______________

352. 18 - 2 = _______________

353. 7 - 1 = _______________

354. 7 - 6 = _______________

355. 8 - 6 = _______________

356. 12 - 11 = _______________

357. 14 - 12 = _______________

358. 12 - 7 = _______________

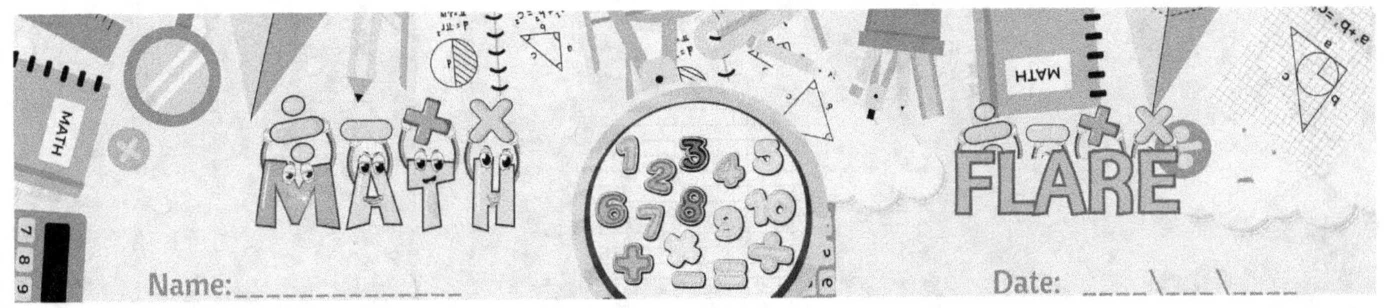

359. 10 - 1 = _______________

360. 18 - 7 = _______________

361. 12 - 10 = _______________

362. 12 - 6 = _______________

363. 17 - 4 = _______________

364. 10 - 4 = _______________

365. 8 - 8 = _______________

366. 18 - 9 = _______________

367. 10 - 5 = _______________

368. 4 - 2 = _______________

369. 18 - 1 = _______________

370. 11 - 4 = _______________

371. 15 - 13 = _______________

372. 13 - 10 = _______________

373. 8 - 3 = _______________

374. 14 - 13 = _______________

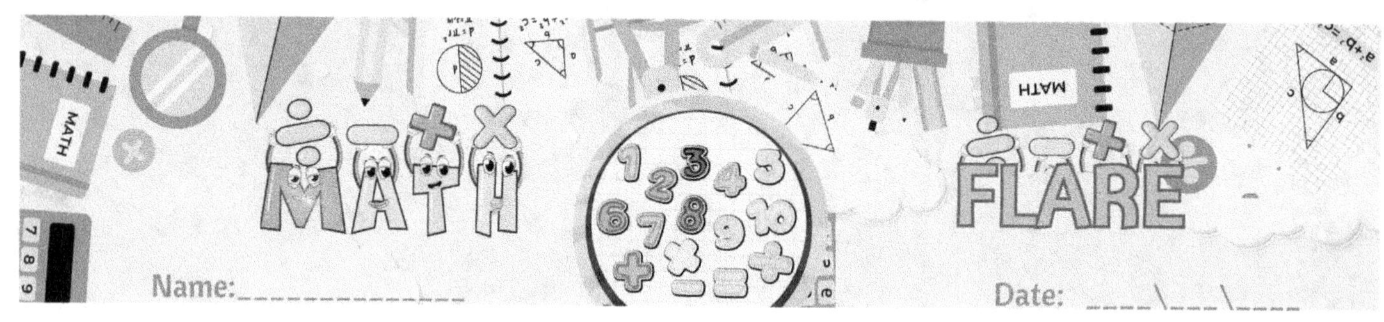

375. 10 - 2 = _______________

376. 8 - 2 = _______________

377. 6 - 1 = _______________

378. 7 - 5 = _______________

379. 20 - 9 = _______________

380. 8 - 4 = _______________

381. 17 - 6 = _______________

382. 8 - 5 = _______________

383. 17 - 1 = _______________

384. 15 - 12 = _______________

385. 19 - 8 = _______________

386. 10 - 10 = _______________

387. 15 - 6 = _______________

388. 10 - 3 = _______________

389. 15 - 9 = _______________

390. 17 - 11 = _______________

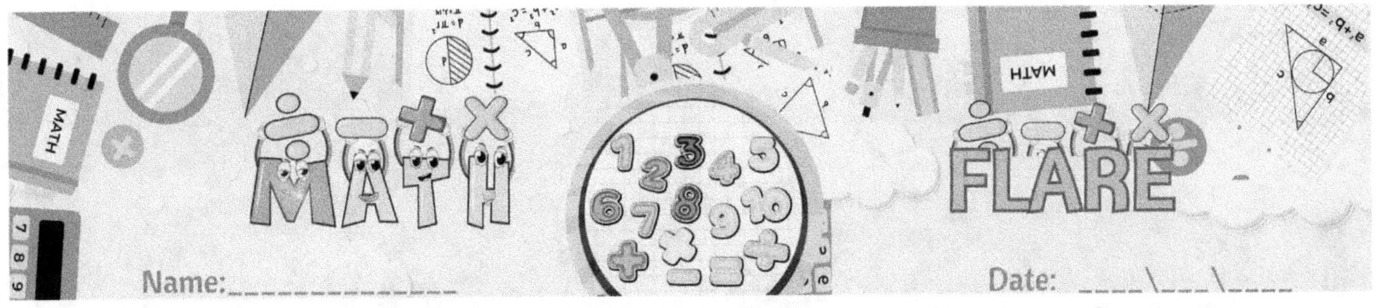

Addition-Subtraction Activities

391.

a. 7 + 5 = _______ •　　　　　• F = 15

b. 10 + 6 = _______ •　　　　　• H = 16

c. 3 + 14 = _______ •　　　　　• A = 0

d. 5 - 3 = _______ •　　　　　• D = 2

e. 1 - 1 = _______ •　　　　　• J = 0

f. 6 - 6 = _______ •　　　　　• C = 22

g. 12 + 3 = _______ •　　　　　• B = 0

h. 2 - 2 = _______ •　　　　　• I = 12

i. 6 + 7 = _______ •　　　　　• G = 13

j. 12 + 10 = _______ •　　　　　• E = 17

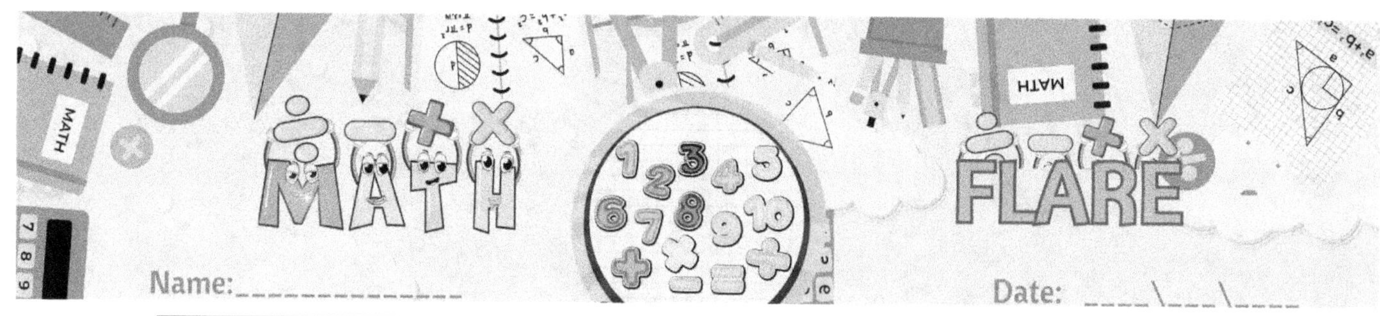

392.

a. 14 + 17 = _______ •	• I = 23
b. 13 − 1 = _______ •	• F = 3
c. 9 − 1 = _______ •	• J = 25
d. 15 − 7 = _______ •	• H = 8
e. 12 + 8 = _______ •	• C = 12
f. 12 + 13 = _______ •	• A = 20
g. 5 + 18 = _______ •	• D = 25
h. 19 + 7 = _______ •	• G = 8
i. 9 + 16 = _______ •	• B = 31
j. 16 − 13 = _______ •	• E = 26

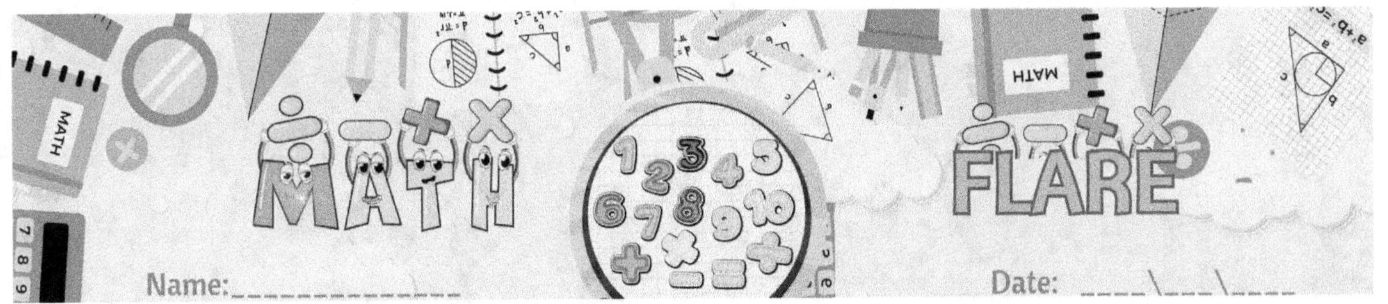

393.

a. 14 + 5 = _______ •	• F = 32
b. 10 + 5 = _______ •	• G = 5
c. 1 - 1 = _______ •	• J = 7
d. 2 + 14 = _______ •	• A = 19
e. 16 - 14 = _______ •	• H = 2
f. 20 + 3 = _______ •	• D = 16
g. 20 + 12 = _______ •	• E = 15
h. 19 + 16 = _______ •	• I = 23
i. 13 - 6 = _______ •	• C = 35
j. 8 - 3 = _______ •	• B = 0

394.

a. 20 + 19 = _______ •	• A = 1
b. 14 + 18 = _______ •	• C = 39
c. 9 – 9 = _______ •	• G = 14
d. 5 – 1 = _______ •	• D = 4
e. 2 + 12 = _______ •	• J = 32
f. 17 + 2 = _______ •	• H = 31
g. 2 – 1 = _______ •	• F = 33
h. 16 + 17 = _______ •	• B = 19
i. 18 + 13 = _______ •	• I = 0
j. 5 + 7 = _______ •	• E = 12

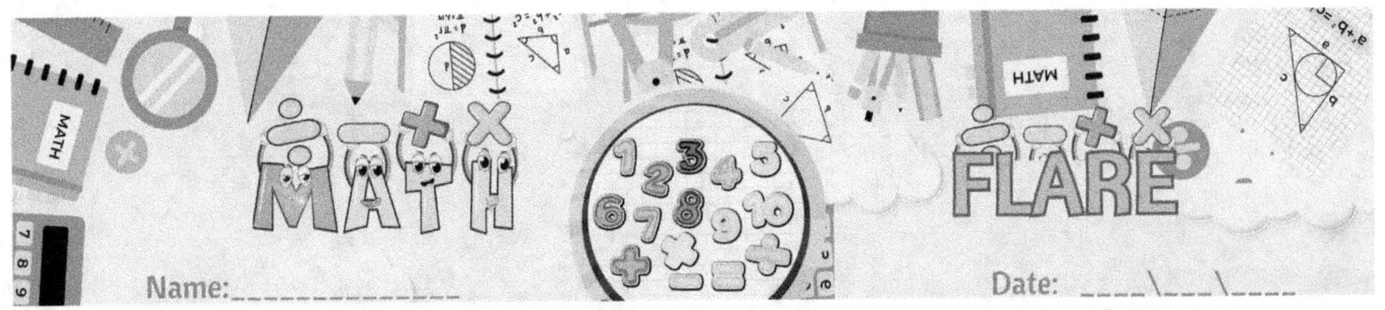

395.

a. 7 + 14 = _______ •   • C = 5

b. 20 - 7 = _______ •   • G = 13

c. 1 - 1 = _______ •   • B = 5

d. 6 - 2 = _______ •   • E = 21

e. 1 + 4 = _______ •   • H = 0

f. 19 - 14 = _______ •   • F = 22

g. 6 - 3 = _______ •   • I = 3

h. 8 + 2 = _______ •   • D = 4

i. 14 + 5 = _______ •   • J = 19

j. 10 + 12 = _______ •   • A = 10

396.

a. 5 - 4 = _______ •	• H = 34
b. 2 - 1 = _______ •	• G = 26
c. 19 - 3 = _______ •	• A = 31
d. 14 + 20 = _______ •	• B = 3
e. 12 - 9 = _______ •	• C = 3
f. 10 - 6 = _______ •	• E = 16
g. 16 + 10 = _______ •	• D = 1
h. 9 - 6 = _______ •	• I = 4
i. 12 + 19 = _______ •	• J = 1
j. 19 + 7 = _______ •	• F = 26

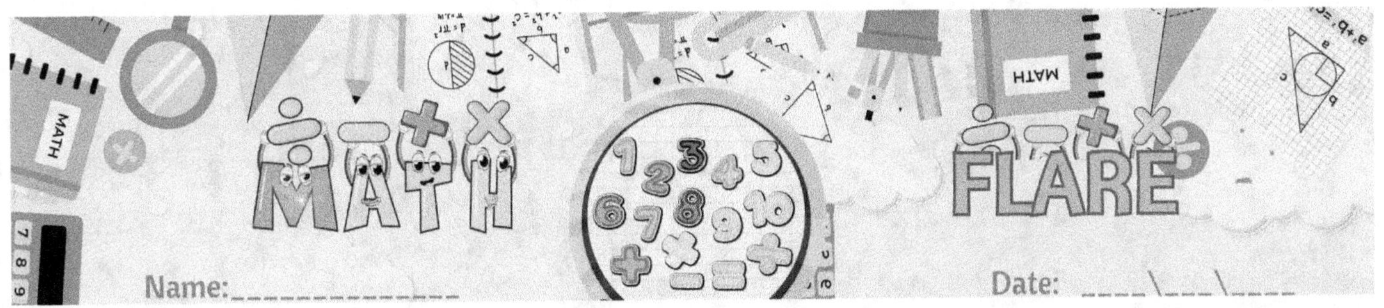

397.

a. 1 + 7 = _______ •	• D = 15
b. 4 + 18 = _______ •	• J = 22
c. 13 − 13 = _______ •	• H = 8
d. 10 + 18 = _______ •	• A = 16
e. 4 + 11 = _______ •	• C = 34
f. 10 − 4 = _______ •	• I = 6
g. 11 + 5 = _______ •	• F = 16
h. 20 + 15 = _______ •	• B = 35
i. 19 + 15 = _______ •	• E = 0
j. 1 + 15 = _______ •	• G = 28

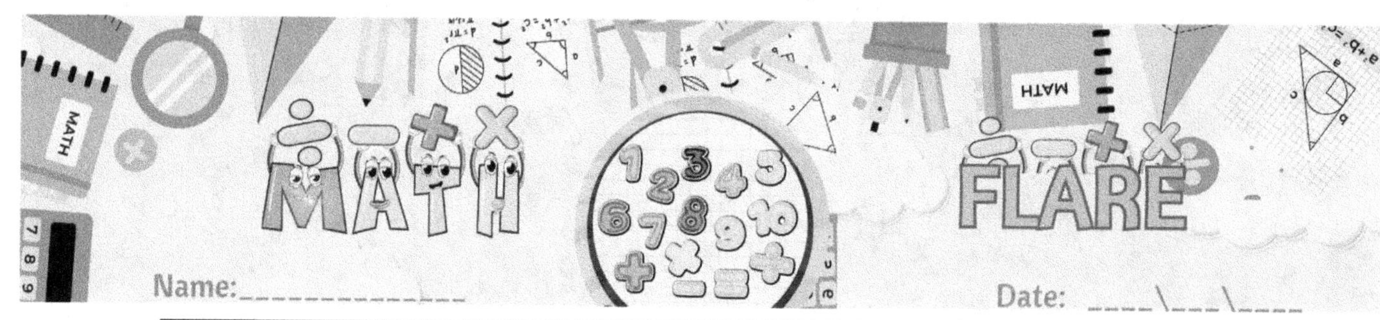

398.

a. 15 + 8 = _____ •	• A = 17
b. 15 - 3 = _____ •	• D = 15
c. 6 + 19 = _____ •	• F = 9
d. 13 + 4 = _____ •	• C = 20
e. 9 + 11 = _____ •	• G = 17
f. 11 - 2 = _____ •	• B = 9
g. 2 + 15 = _____ •	• H = 25
h. 16 - 7 = _____ •	• I = 20
i. 18 - 3 = _____ •	• E = 23
j. 12 + 8 = _____ •	• J = 12

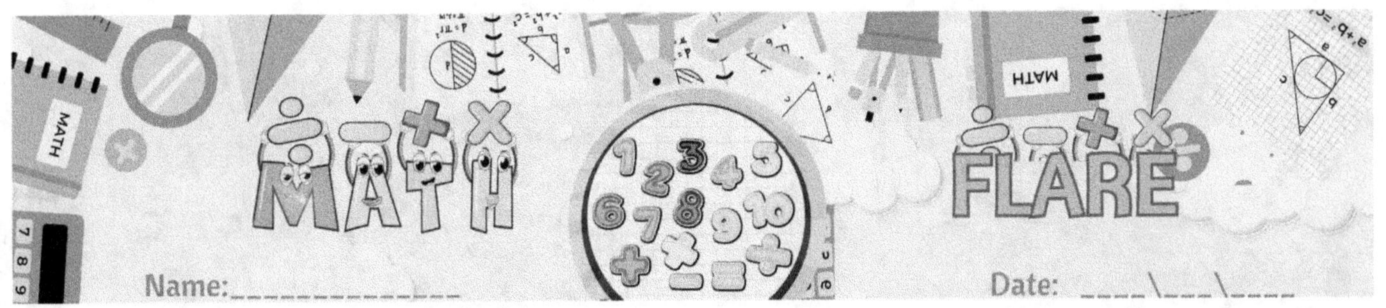

399.

a. 3 + 18 = _______ •	• G = 8
b. 17 + 8 = _______ •	• A = 0
c. 10 + 5 = _______ •	• F = 25
d. 19 - 1 = _______ •	• H = 21
e. 12 - 4 = _______ •	• D = 15
f. 8 - 7 = _______ •	• I = 25
g. 12 - 12 = _______ •	• J = 27
h. 20 + 7 = _______ •	• C = 18
i. 12 + 1 = _______ •	• B = 13
j. 8 + 17 = _______ •	• E = 1

Name:___________________   Date: _______________

400.

a. 19 + 8 = _______   •   • E = 27

b. 15 - 9 = _______   •   • A = 10

c. 12 + 3 = _______   •   • I = 23

d. 14 - 4 = _______   •   • G = 23

e. 11 + 18 = _______   •   • H = 5

f. 15 - 1 = _______   •   • C = 29

g. 9 + 14 = _______   •   • J = 6

h. 17 + 6 = _______   •   • B = 15

i. 17 - 7 = _______   •   • F = 10

j. 2 + 3 = _______   •   • D = 14

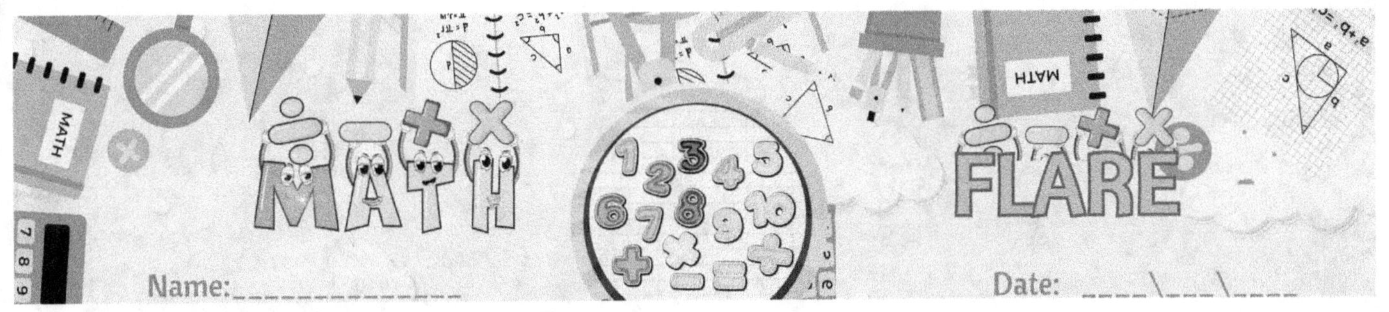

Addition: 1 through 100

Find the Sum.

401. 42 + 81	402. 8 + 91	403. 23 + 49	404. 74 + 17
405. 4 + 61	406. 26 + 92	407. 9 + 1	408. 97 + 74
409. 42 + 89	410. 2 + 34	411. 1 + 28	412. 25 + 47
413. 8 + 76	414. 63 + 45	415. 96 + 24	416. 34 + 63

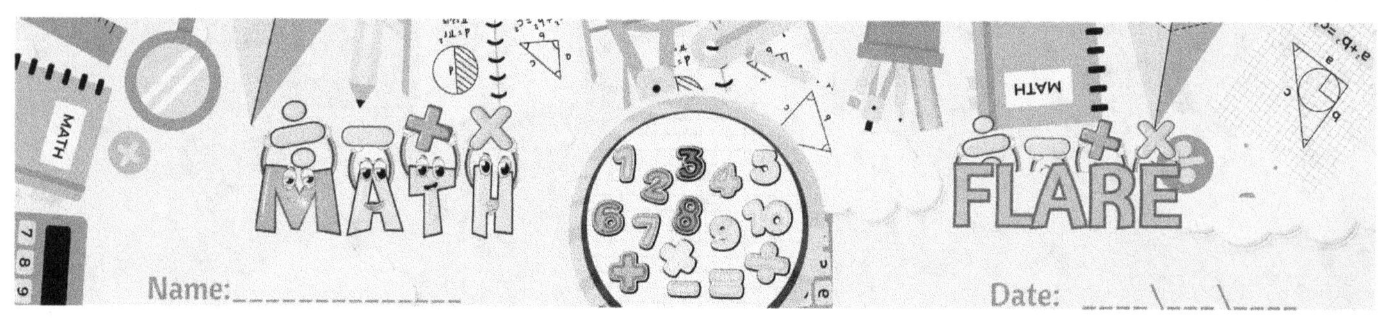

417.	2 + 69	418.	78 + 61	419.	92 + 28	420.	34 + 83
421.	52 + 28	422.	73 + 89	423.	38 + 15	424.	55 + 71
425.	84 + 93	426.	41 + 62	427.	51 + 15	428.	85 + 15
429.	57 + 61	430.	84 + 47	431.	86 + 30	432.	20 + 80
433.	28 + 63	434.	91 + 41	435.	23 + 38	436.	82 + 14

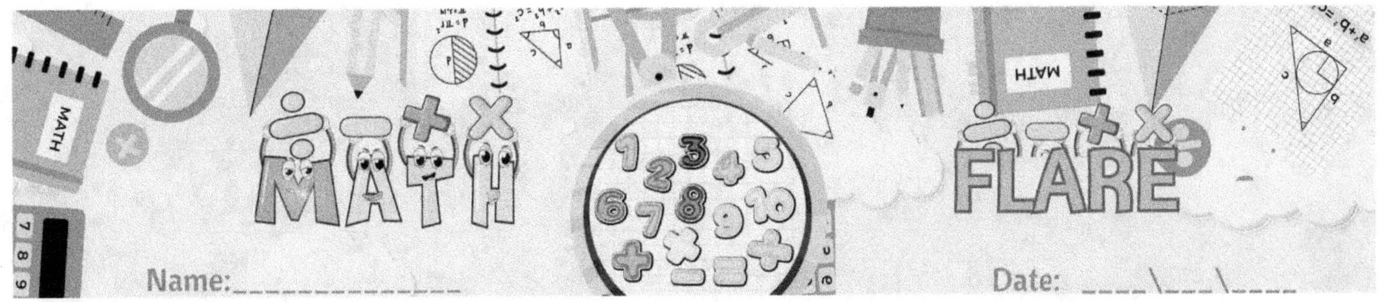

437. 56 + 19	438. 82 + 74	439. 55 + 37	440. 10 + 93
441. 22 + 92	442. 61 + 4	443. 82 + 72	444. 13 + 87
445. 84 + 64	446. 5 + 31	447. 45 + 87	448. 97 + 23
449. 8 + 93	450. 62 + 75	451. 24 + 15	452. 49 + 47
453. 12 + 28	454. 7 + 33	455. 32 + 12	456. 60 + 21

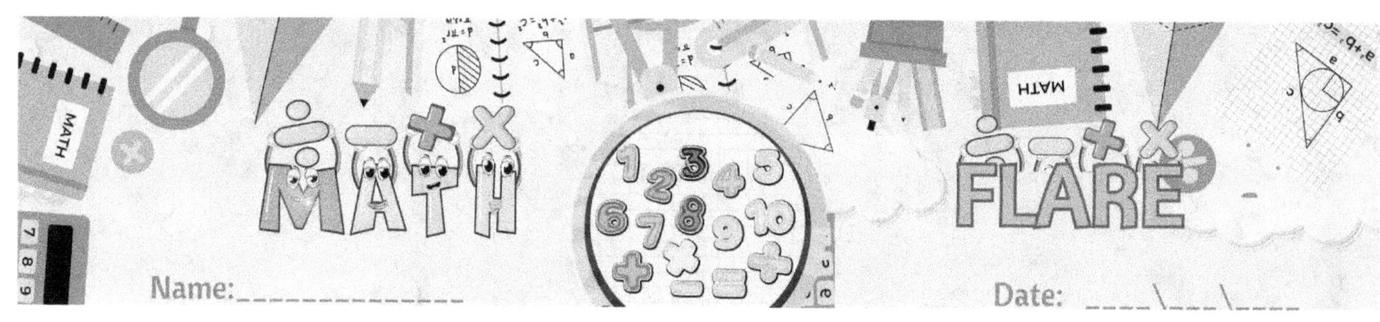

457. 52 + 90	458. 25 + 93	459. 69 + 17	460. 98 + 55
461. 50 + 4	462. 57 + 59	463. 33 + 52	464. 69 + 69
465. 22 + 60	466. 66 + 62	467. 75 + 35	468. 70 + 8
469. 45 + 15	470. 92 + 56	471. 67 + 80	472. 56 + 73
473. 5 + 84	474. 79 + 55	475. 63 + 5	476. 54 + 91

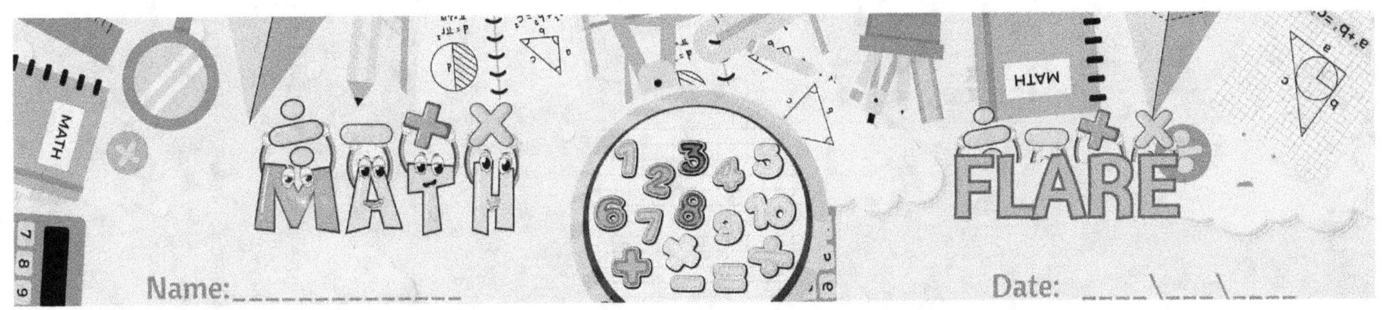

477. $\quad 95$ $+ \quad 8$	478. $\quad 26$ $+ \ 21$	479. $\quad 58$ $+ \ 89$	480. $\quad 15$ $+ \ 60$
481. $\quad 58$ $+ \ 38$	482. $\quad 13$ $+ \ 72$	483. $\quad 46$ $+ \ 98$	484. $\quad 46$ $+ \ 19$
485. $\quad 21$ $+ \ 18$	486. $\quad 49$ $+ \ 54$	487. $\quad 25$ $+ \ 43$	488. $\quad 89$ $+ \ 71$
489. $\quad 48$ $+ \ 84$	490. $\quad 56$ $+ \ 49$	491. $\quad 73$ $+ \ 16$	492. $\quad 7$ $+ \ 17$
493. $\quad 7$ $+ \ 76$	494. $\quad 67$ $+ \ 68$	495. $\quad 10$ $+ \ 50$	496. $\quad 50$ $+ \ 56$

Subtraction: 1 through 100

Find the Difference.

497.	498.	499.	500.
11 − 4	97 − 29	71 − 59	35 − 3

501.	502.	503.	504.
45 − 28	40 − 19	60 − 1	70 − 37

505.	506.	507.	508.
27 − 15	75 − 56	40 − 27	88 − 39

509.	510.	511.	512.
38 − 36	69 − 48	38 − 30	19 − 14

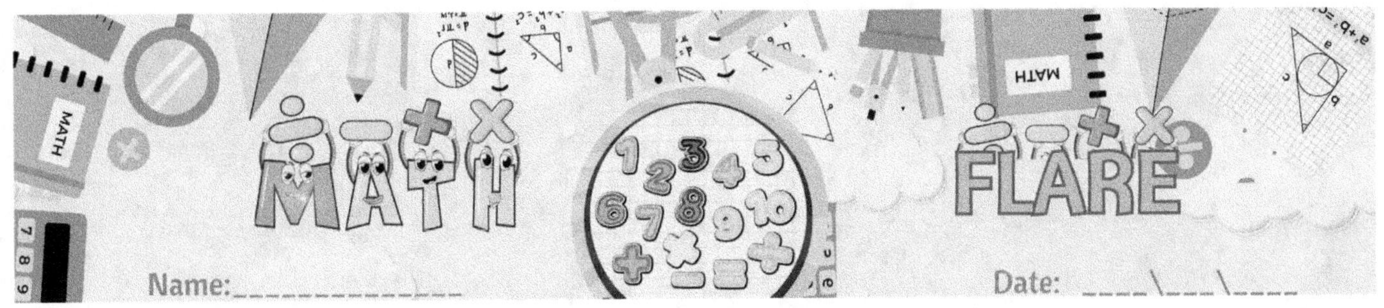

| 513. | 71
− 66 | 514. | 58
− 53 | 515. | 51
− 31 | 516. | 13
− 9 |

517. 61 − 31   518. 19 − 3   519. 83 − 51   520. 65 − 5

521. 18 − 3   522. 54 − 29   523. 79 − 60   524. 29 − 11

525. 52 − 29   526. 98 − 71   527. 26 − 15   528. 77 − 47

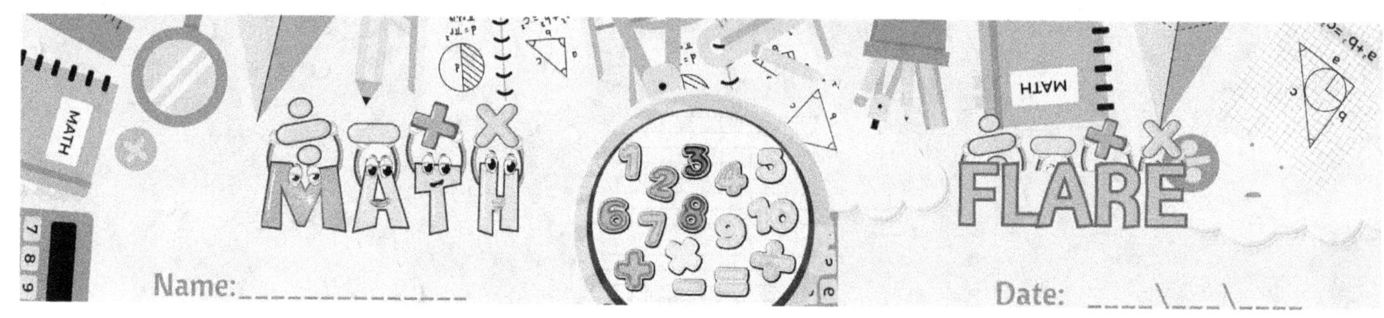

529.　　56 　　− 36	530.　　80 　　− 50	531.　　52 　　− 39	532.　　16 　　− 10
533.　　57 　　−　6	534.　　26 　　− 22	535.　　60 　　− 44	536.　　66 　　− 47
537.　　41 　　− 25	538.　　65 　　− 12	539.　　37 　　− 21	540.　　95 　　− 88
541.　　75 　　− 14	542.　　51 　　− 47	543.　　66 　　− 21	544.　　52 　　− 52

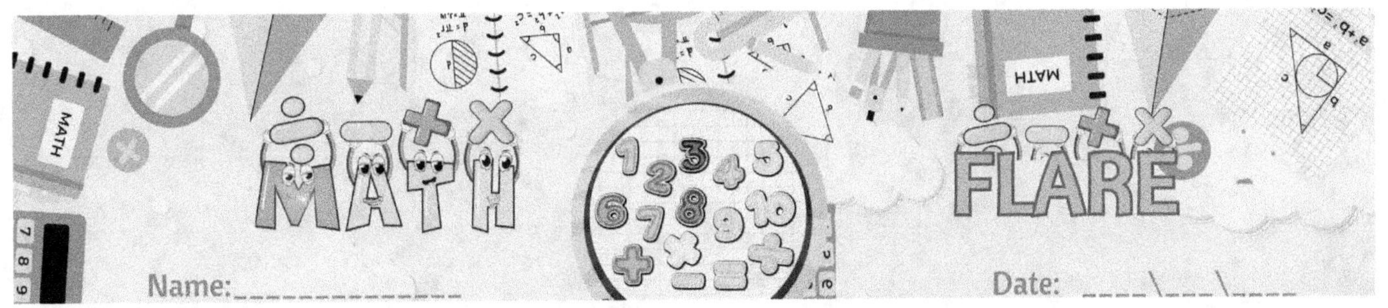

545. 78 − 40	546. 66 − 13	547. 85 − 84	548. 63 − 23
549. 16 − 14	550. 12 − 9	551. 62 − 24	552. 82 − 60
553. 93 − 26	554. 44 − 26	555. 97 − 55	556. 37 − 35
557. 72 − 62	558. 91 − 27	559. 35 − 6	560. 98 − 21

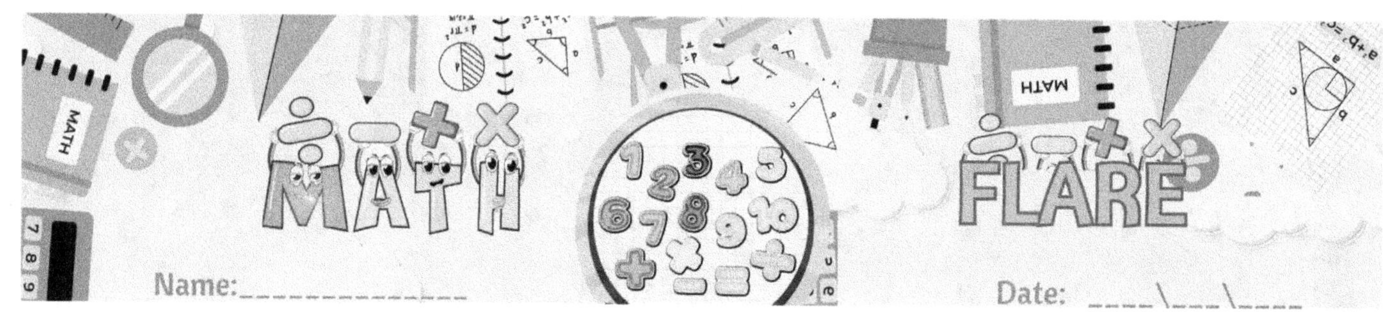

561. $\begin{array}{r} 65 \\ -\ 13 \\ \hline \end{array}$	562. $\begin{array}{r} 17 \\ -\ 2 \\ \hline \end{array}$	563. $\begin{array}{r} 21 \\ -\ 10 \\ \hline \end{array}$	564. $\begin{array}{r} 89 \\ -\ 32 \\ \hline \end{array}$
565. $\begin{array}{r} 20 \\ -\ 9 \\ \hline \end{array}$	566. $\begin{array}{r} 59 \\ -\ 16 \\ \hline \end{array}$	567. $\begin{array}{r} 41 \\ -\ 15 \\ \hline \end{array}$	568. $\begin{array}{r} 44 \\ -\ 33 \\ \hline \end{array}$
569. $\begin{array}{r} 100 \\ -\ 35 \\ \hline \end{array}$	570. $\begin{array}{r} 94 \\ -\ 84 \\ \hline \end{array}$	571. $\begin{array}{r} 12 \\ -\ 3 \\ \hline \end{array}$	572. $\begin{array}{r} 28 \\ -\ 19 \\ \hline \end{array}$
573. $\begin{array}{r} 55 \\ -\ 53 \\ \hline \end{array}$	574. $\begin{array}{r} 18 \\ -\ 6 \\ \hline \end{array}$	575. $\begin{array}{r} 16 \\ -\ 15 \\ \hline \end{array}$	576. $\begin{array}{r} 93 \\ -\ 75 \\ \hline \end{array}$

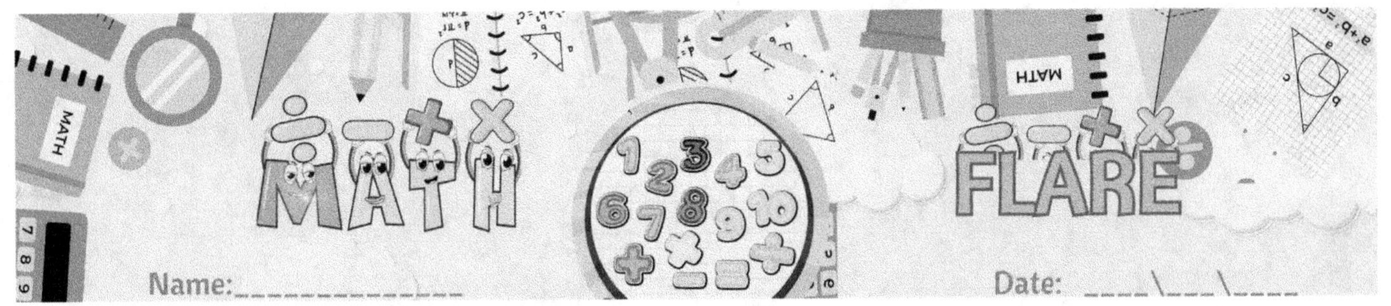

577. 16 − 7	578. 36 − 27	579. 65 − 32	580. 46 − 2
581. 60 − 43	582. 51 − 46	583. 47 − 21	584. 57 − 32
585. 92 − 51	586. 25 − 16	587. 35 − 26	588. 24 − 21
589. 87 − 40	590. 94 − 85	591. 34 − 25	592. 27 − 6

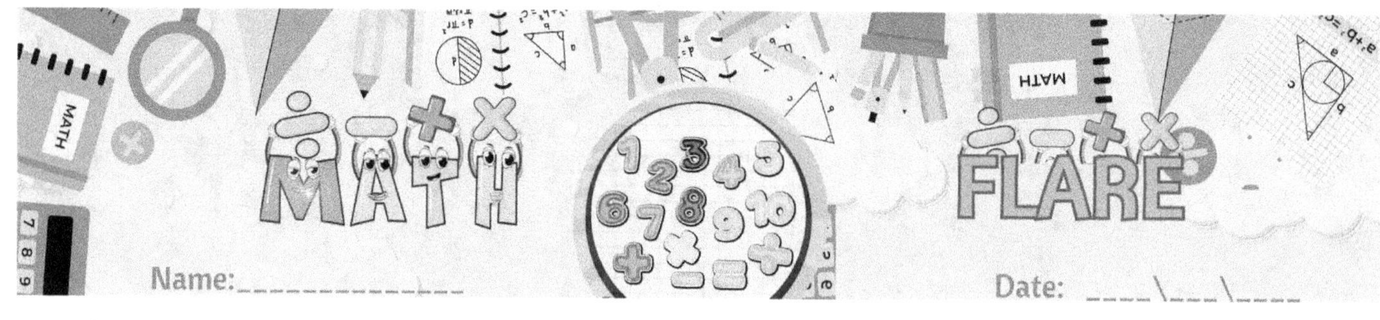

Addition with Regrouping

Find the sum.

593. 48 + 74	594. 19 + 94	595. 6 + 64	596. 13 + 99
597. 95 + 95	598. 34 + 78	599. 75 + 39	600. 26 + 7
601. 46 + 64	602. 41 + 69	603. 75 + 37	604. 53 + 77
605. 25 + 89	606. 89 + 57	607. 55 + 56	608. 75 + 85
609. 53 + 78	610. 43 + 68	611. 26 + 88	612. 51 + 59

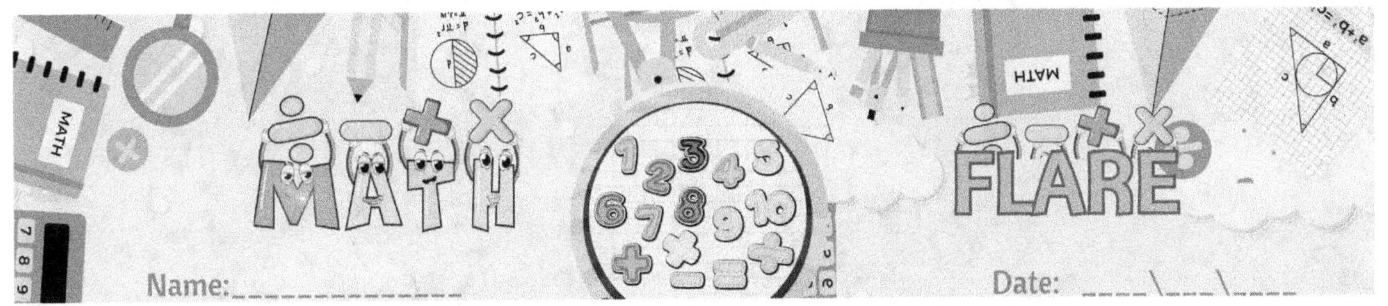

Name: ___________________ Date: _______________

613. 43 + 69	614. 68 + 77	615. 39 + 85	616. 15 + 96
617. 21 + 89	618. 45 + 76	619. 32 + 88	620. 46 + 88
621. 71 + 69	622. 75 + 97	623. 96 + 46	624. 17 + 93
625. 79 + 56	626. 87 + 58	627. 81 + 89	628. 4 + 17
629. 11 + 99	630. 63 + 68	631. 97 + 49	632. 28 + 94

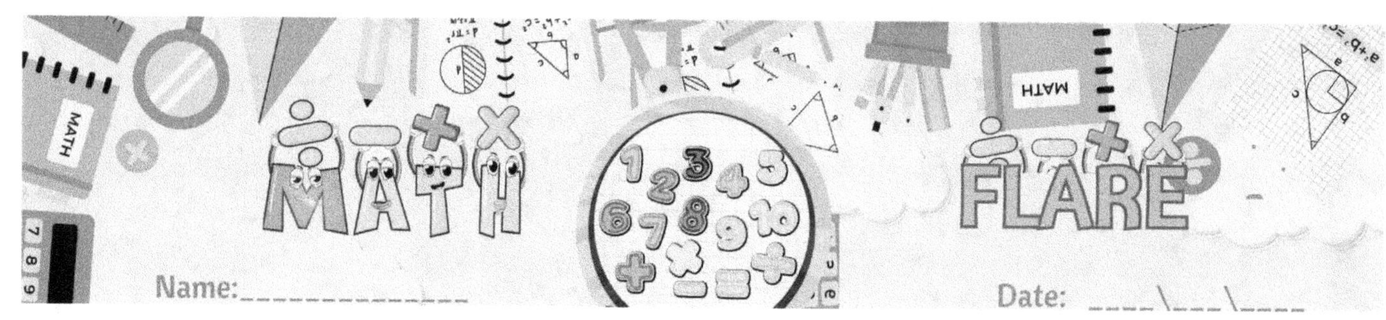

633. 96 + 68	634. 5 + 7	635. 53 + 89	636. 81 + 29
637. 48 + 73	638. 87 + 86	639. 53 + 67	640. 71 + 79
641. 7 + 65	642. 8 + 58	643. 71 + 59	644. 58 + 86
645. 56 + 4	646. 87 + 33	647. 38 + 72	648. 1 + 29
649. 42 + 68	650. 96 + 94	651. 69 + 62	652. 2 + 18

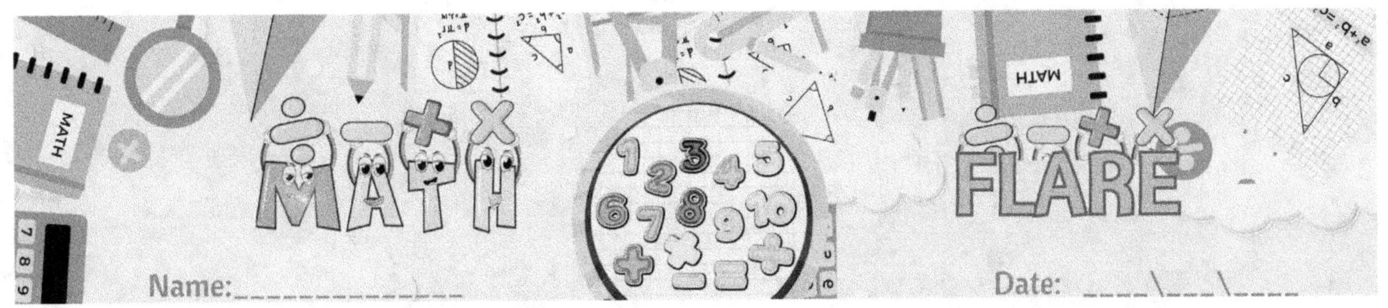

653.	654.	655.	656.
61 + 69	41 + 99	97 + 8	33 + 89

657.	658.	659.	660.
64 + 98	61 + 49	28 + 85	71 + 49

661.	662.	663.	664.
56 + 56	46 + 69	81 + 9	93 + 17

665.	666.	667.	668.
96 + 9	52 + 69	57 + 54	59 + 95

669.	670.	671.	672.
95 + 16	7 + 79	99 + 75	78 + 66

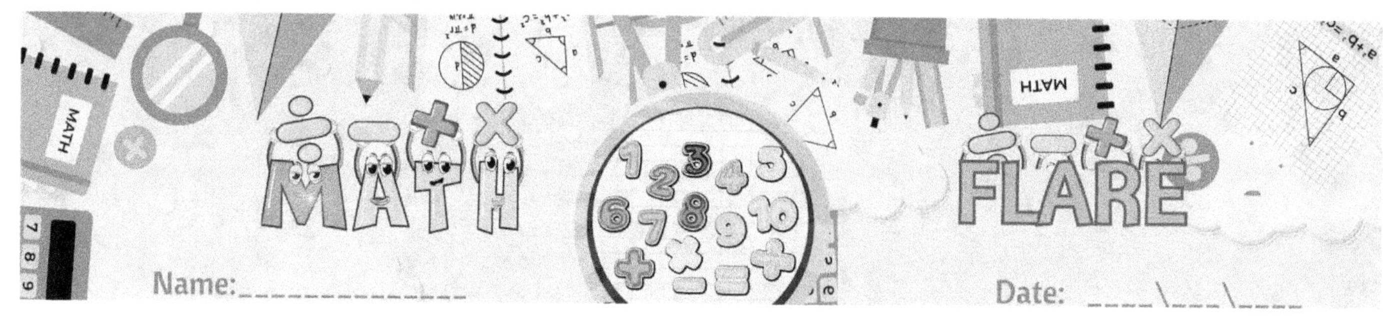

673. 68 + 94	674. 84 + 68	675. 67 + 95	676. 91 + 69
677. 83 + 47	678. 68 + 59	679. 18 + 99	680. 61 + 99
681. 15 + 97	682. 67 + 56	683. 83 + 97	684. 91 + 79
685. 39 + 77	686. 58 + 75	687. 33 + 88	688. 73 + 87
689. 21 + 99	690. 47 + 76	691. 18 + 96	692. 86 + 64

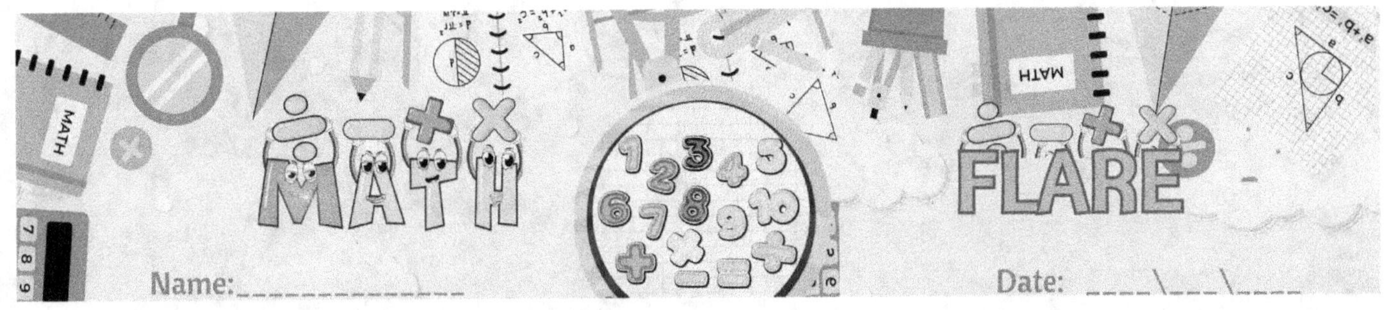

Subtraction with Regrouping

Find the difference.

693.   80
    − 9
	694. 70
	    − 67
		695. 50
		    − 7
			696. 60
			    − 47

697.   8
    − 3
	698. 80
	    − 61
		699. 4
		    − 1
			700. 80
			    − 28

701.   70
    − 26
	702. 20
	    − 2
		703. 80
		    − 75
			704. 10
			    − 4

705.   20
    − 15
	706. 70
	    − 59
		707. 30
		    − 3
			708. 70
			    − 65

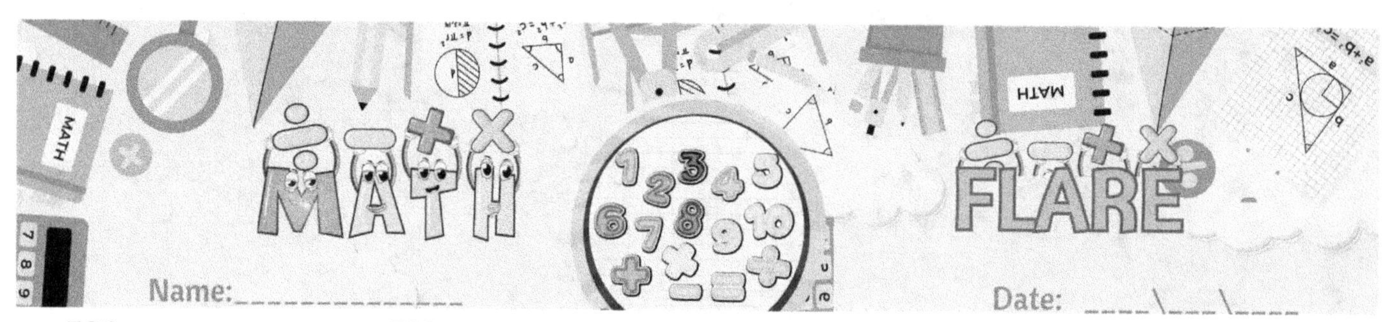

709. $\begin{array}{r} 60 \\ -\ 33 \\ \hline \end{array}$	710. $\begin{array}{r} 50 \\ -\ 13 \\ \hline \end{array}$	711. $\begin{array}{r} 10 \\ -\ 7 \\ \hline \end{array}$	712. $\begin{array}{r} 20 \\ -\ 12 \\ \hline \end{array}$
713. $\begin{array}{r} 90 \\ -\ 75 \\ \hline \end{array}$	714. $\begin{array}{r} 10 \\ -\ 5 \\ \hline \end{array}$	715. $\begin{array}{r} 20 \\ -\ 11 \\ \hline \end{array}$	716. $\begin{array}{r} 80 \\ -\ 47 \\ \hline \end{array}$
717. $\begin{array}{r} 70 \\ -\ 18 \\ \hline \end{array}$	718. $\begin{array}{r} 90 \\ -\ 84 \\ \hline \end{array}$	719. $\begin{array}{r} 40 \\ -\ 28 \\ \hline \end{array}$	720. $\begin{array}{r} 80 \\ -\ 33 \\ \hline \end{array}$
721. $\begin{array}{r} 80 \\ -\ 5 \\ \hline \end{array}$	722. $\begin{array}{r} 20 \\ -\ 4 \\ \hline \end{array}$	723. $\begin{array}{r} 20 \\ -\ 16 \\ \hline \end{array}$	724. $\begin{array}{r} 20 \\ -\ 8 \\ \hline \end{array}$

725. 40 − 13	726. 80 − 48	727. 40 − 25	728. 100 − 58
729. 30 − 9	730. 50 − 1	731. 70 − 11	732. 80 − 13
733. 80 − 26	734. 70 − 39	735. 20 − 3	736. 1 − 1
737. 50 − 42	738. 80 − 32	739. 90 − 73	740. 30 − 14

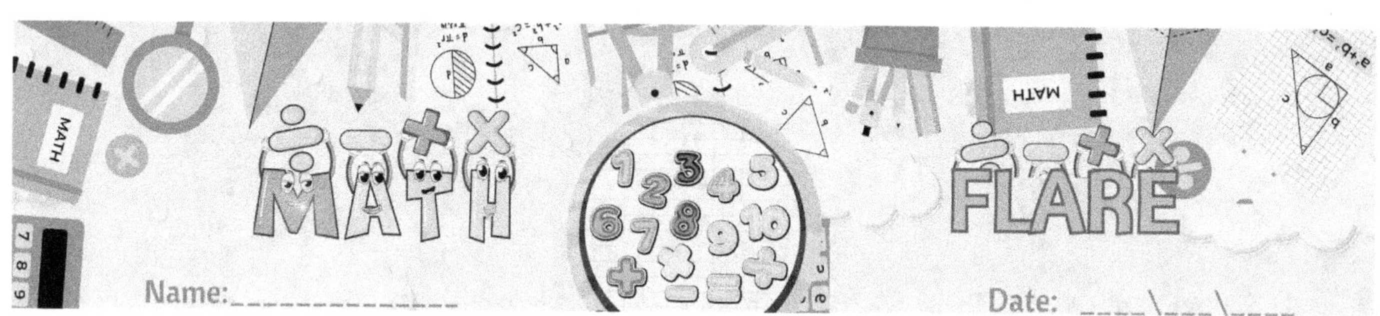

741. 10 − 3	742. 50 − 21	743. 50 − 33	744. 30 − 7
745. 30 − 21	746. 3 − 2	747. 80 − 35	748. 40 − 15
749. 40 − 9	750. 5 − 2	751. 40 − 24	752. 80 − 72
753. 80 − 55	754. 60 − 23	755. 90 − 5	756. 60 − 14

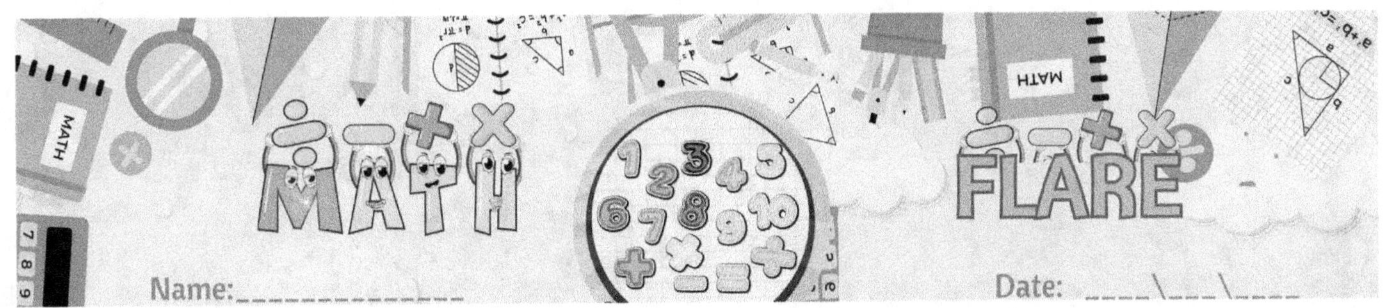

757.	758.	759.	760.
10 - 2	80 - 11	60 - 19	70 - 46

761.	762.	763.	764.
50 - 46	2 - 1	80 - 58	60 - 53

765.	766.	767.	768.
90 - 41	40 - 33	40 - 4	70 - 19

769.	770.	771.	772.
50 - 43	90 - 79	60 - 7	3 - 1

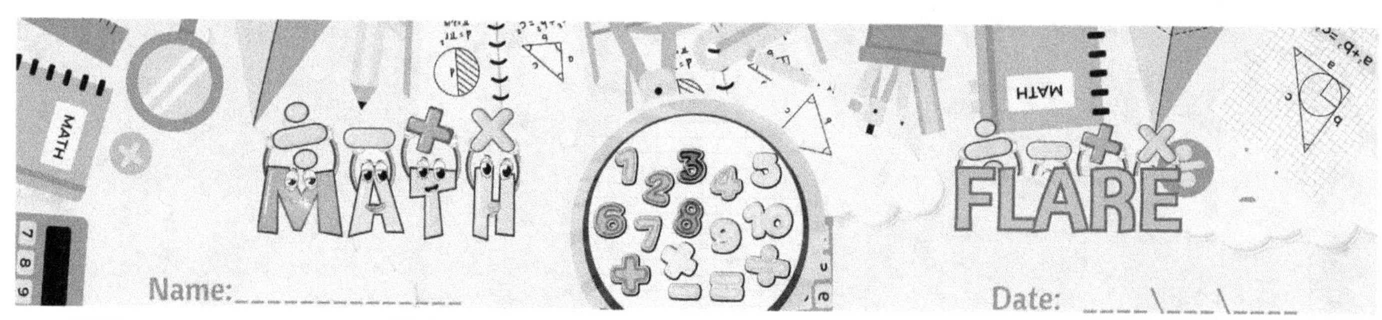

773. 50
    − 38
    ______

774. 60
    − 13
    ______

775. 90
    − 19
    ______

776. 60
    − 34
    ______

777. 90
    − 17
    ______

778. 70
    − 27
    ______

779. 80
    −   1
    ______

780. 80
    − 37
    ______

781. 30
    − 22
    ______

782. 90
    − 72
    ______

783. 60
    − 32
    ______

784. 40
    − 18
    ______

785. 70
    − 15
    ______

786. 70
    − 43
    ______

787. 50
    − 44
    ______

788. 30
    − 17
    ______

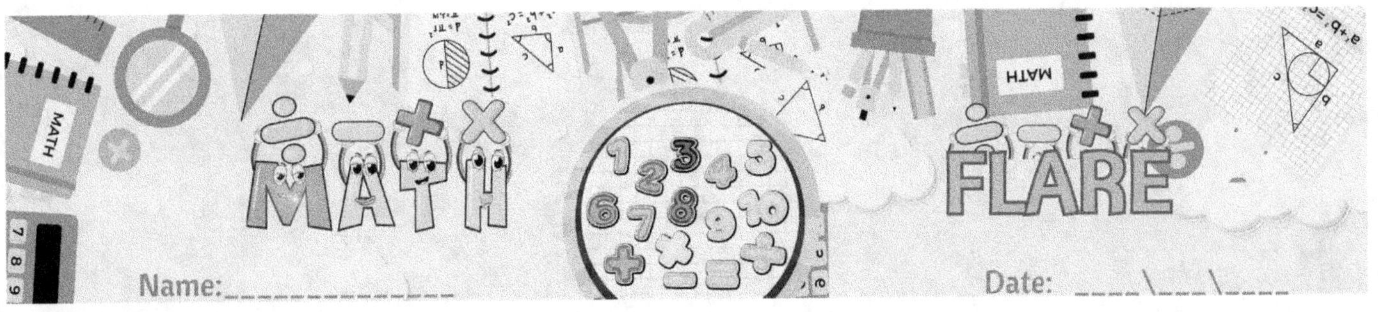

Make 100

Add a number to the first number to make 100.

789. $58 + \underline{\quad} = 100$

790. $68 + \underline{\quad} = 100$

791. $13 + \underline{\quad} = 100$

792. $73 + \underline{\quad} = 100$

793. $19 + \underline{\quad} = 100$

794. $74 + \underline{\quad} = 100$

795. $56 + \underline{\quad} = 100$

796. $97 + \underline{\quad} = 100$

797. $15 + \underline{\quad} = 100$

798. $45 + \underline{\quad} = 100$

799. $10 + \underline{\quad} = 100$

800. $3 + \underline{\quad} = 100$

801. $86 + \underline{\quad} = 100$

802. $25 + \underline{\quad} = 100$

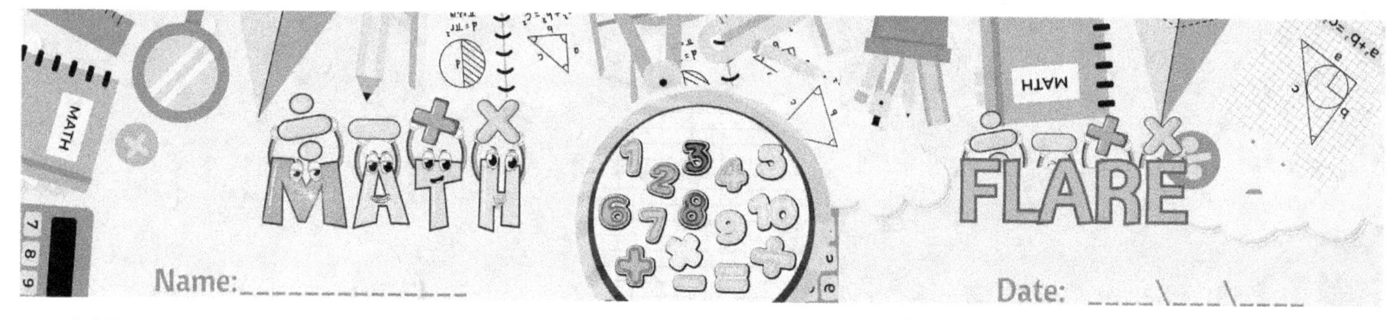

803. 95 + ___ = 100

804. 99 + ___ = 100

805. 35 + ___ = 100

806. 31 + ___ = 100

807. 18 + ___ = 100

808. 88 + ___ = 100

809. 24 + ___ = 100

810. 75 + ___ = 100

811. 41 + ___ = 100

812. 87 + ___ = 100

813. 6 + ___ = 100

814. 70 + ___ = 100

815. 4 + ___ = 100

816. 94 + ___ = 100

817. 67 + ___ = 100

818. 49 + ___ = 100

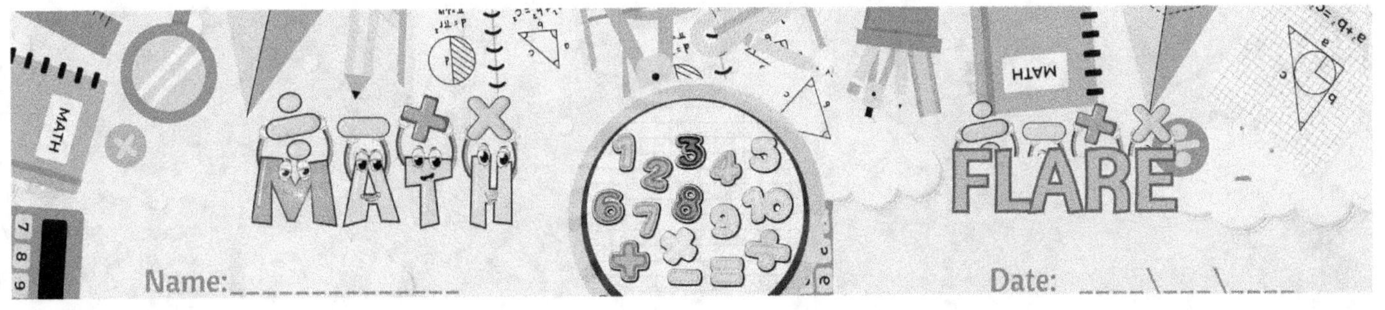

819. 93 + __ = 100

820. 91 + __ = 100

821. 40 + ___ = 100

822. 7 + ___ = 100

823. 28 + ___ = 100

824. 12 + ___ = 100

825. 89 + __ = 100

826. 16 + ___ = 100

827. 33 + ___ = 100

828. 54 + ___ = 100

829. 46 + ___ = 100

830. 23 + ___ = 100

831. 53 + ___ = 100

832. 17 + ___ = 100

833. 1 + ___ = 100

834. 71 + ___ = 100

835. 65 + ___ = 100

836. 37 + ___ = 100

837. 43 + ___ = 100

838. 32 + ___ = 100

839. 42 + ___ = 100

840. 76 + ___ = 100

841. 39 + ___ = 100

842. 66 + ___ = 100

843. 85 + ___ = 100

844. 22 + ___ = 100

845. 69 + ___ = 100

846. 72 + ___ = 100

847. 21 + ___ = 100

848. 80 + ___ = 100

849. 77 + ___ = 100

850. 5 + ___ = 100

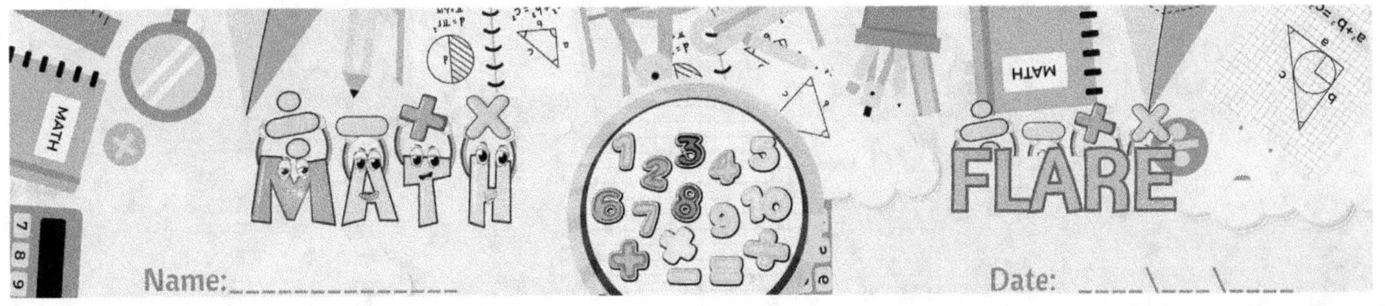

851. 26 + ___ = 100

852. 51 + ___ = 100

853. 92 + ___ = 100

854. 83 + ___ = 100

855. 64 + ___ = 100

856. 55 + ___ = 100

857. 63 + ___ = 100

858. 60 + ___ = 100

859. 14 + ___ = 100

860. 78 + ___ = 100

861. 57 + ___ = 100

862. 62 + ___ = 100

863. 36 + ___ = 100

864. 9 + ___ = 100

865. 100 + ___ = 100

866. 59 + ___ = 100

867. 82 + ___ = 100

868. 90 + ___ = 100

869. 27 + ___ = 100

870. 61 + ___ = 100

871. 50 + ___ = 100

872. 11 + ___ = 100

873. 30 + ___ = 100

874. 79 + ___ = 100

875. 20 + ___ = 100

876. 29 + ___ = 100

877. 8 + ___ = 100

878. 34 + ___ = 100

879. 84 + ___ = 100

880. 38 + ___ = 100

881. 48 + ___ = 100

882. 2 + ___ = 100

ANSWERS

Page 1:   Addition: 1 through 20

1. 15	2. 25	3. 13	4. 17	5. 12	6. 9	7. 9	8. 27
9. 15	10. 17	11. 17	12. 24	13. 11	14. 28	15. 16	16. 32
17. 22	18. 14	19. 10	20. 16	21. 28	22. 21	23. 23	24. 28
25. 21	26. 15	27. 10	28. 39	29. 25	30. 20	31. 16	32. 16
33. 14	34. 32	35. 3	36. 14	37. 7	38. 17	39. 32	40. 22
41. 20	42. 21	43. 15	44. 20	45. 20	46. 24	47. 36	48. 11
49. 25	50. 30	51. 18	52. 28	53. 26	54. 9	55. 33	56. 25
57. 9	58. 7	59. 21	60. 19	61. 33	62. 31	63. 18	64. 10
65. 23	66. 25	67. 29	68. 25	69. 5	70. 30	71. 25	72. 12
73. 16	74. 24	75. 15	76. 8	77. 30	78. 20	79. 12	80. 25
81. 17	82. 22	83. 22	84. 17	85. 29	86. 22	87. 17	88. 33
89. 16	90. 24	91. 28	92. 14	93. 6	94. 34	95. 15	96. 19
97. 17	98. 24	99. 21	100. 31				

Page 6:   Addition: 1 through 20

101. 37	102. 15	103. 25	104. 25	105. 15	106. 19	107. 19	108. 15
109. 21	110. 31	111. 10	112. 14	113. 28	114. 13	115. 9	116. 14
117. 14	118. 30	119. 21	120. 27	121. 8	122. 29	123. 11	124. 15
125. 17	126. 20	127. 24	128. 21	129. 8	130. 16	131. 17	132. 18
133. 29	134. 22	135. 20	136. 23	137. 26	138. 32	139. 31	140. 8

141. 31   142. 28   143. 26   144. 10   145. 22   146. 4   147. 24   148. 19

149. 10   150. 33   151. 25   152. 24   153. 27   154. 39   155. 21   156. 30

157. 12   158. 23   159. 11   160. 18   161. 23   162. 30   163. 19   164. 4

165. 23   166. 7   167. 23   168. 5   169. 22   170. 12   171. 7   172. 14

173. 7   174. 20   175. 17   176. 21   177. 26   178. 26   179. 14   180. 13

181. 27   182. 28   183. 21   184. 15   185. 28   186. 14   187. 32   188. 19

189. 33   190. 33   191. 30   192. 3   193. 24   194. 10   195. 30   196. 34

Page 13: Subtraction: 1 through 20

197. 4   198. 1   199. 13   200. 5   201. 2   202. 2   203. 6   204. 16

205. 7   206. 8   207. 15   208. 6   209. 5   210. 3   211. 14   212. 1

213. 0   214. 3   215. 13   216. 1   217. 4   218. 10   219. 1   220. 1

221. 2   222. 15   223. 0   224. 7   225. 4   226. 5   227. 13   228. 5

229. 8   230. 7   231. 4   232. 4   233. 4   234. 11   235. 9   236. 7

237. 1   238. 6   239. 3   240. 0   241. 3   242. 4   243. 4   244. 7

245. 7   246. 12   247. 0   248. 7   249. 7   250. 2   251. 5   252. 8

253. 9   254. 4   255. 12   256. 0   257. 1   258. 8   259. 10   260. 1

261. 9   262. 3   263. 1   264. 3   265. 7   266. 1   267. 4   268. 2

269. 7   270. 4   271. 5   272. 2   273. 17   274. 2   275. 0   276. 15

277. 8   278. 2   279. 1   280. 2   281. 1   282. 2   283. 14   284. 1

285. 2   286. 6   287. 15   288. 7   289. 3   290. 5   291. 12   292. 3

293. 6   294. 2   295. 11   296. 1

Page 18: Subtraction: 1 through 20

297. 0	298. 1	299. 0	300. 8	301. 5	302. 0	303. 2	304. 6
305. 13	306. 3	307. 2	308. 1	309. 5	310. 7	311. 7	312. 15
313. 3	314. 3	315. 3	316. 0	317. 8	318. 12	319. 3	320. 15
321. 1	322. 8	323. 10	324. 0	325. 9	326. 0	327. 3	328. 4
329. 4	330. 1	331. 14	332. 6	333. 4	334. 11	335. 2	336. 10
337. 12	338. 1	339. 4	340. 4	341. 5	342. 4	343. 8	344. 4
345. 1	346. 0	347. 7	348. 3	349. 16	350. 17	351. 0	352. 16
353. 6	354. 1	355. 2	356. 1	357. 2	358. 5	359. 9	360. 11
361. 2	362. 6	363. 13	364. 6	365. 0	366. 9	367. 5	368. 2
369. 17	370. 7	371. 2	372. 3	373. 5	374. 1	375. 8	376. 6
377. 5	378. 2	379. 11	380. 4	381. 11	382. 3	383. 16	384. 3
385. 11	386. 0	387. 9	388. 7	389. 6	390. 6		

Page 24: Addition-Subtraction Activities

391. a.I b.H c.E d.D e.J f.A g.F h.B i.G j.C

392. a.B b.C c.G d.H e.A f.J g.I h.E i.D j.F

393. a.A b.E c.B d.D e.H f.I g.F h.C i.J j.G

394. a.C b.J c.I d.D e.G f.B g.A h.F i.H j.E

395. a.E b.G c.H d.D e.B f.C g.I h.A i.J j.F

396. a.D b.J c.E d.H e.C f.I g.G h.B i.A j.F

397. a.H b.J c.E d.G e.D f.I g.A h.B i.C j.F

398. a.E b.J c.H d.A e.C f.F g.G h.B i.D j.I

399. a.H b.F c.D d.C e.G f.E g.A h.J i.B j.I

400. a.E b.J c.B d.F e.C f.D g.G h.I i.A j.H

Page 34: Addition: 1 through 100

401. 123	402. 99	403. 72	404. 91	405. 65	406. 118
407. 10	408. 171	409. 131	410. 36	411. 29	412. 72
413. 84	414. 108	415. 120	416. 97	417. 71	418. 139
419. 120	420. 117	421. 80	422. 162	423. 53	424. 126
425. 177	426. 103	427. 66	428. 100	429. 118	430. 131
431. 116	432. 100	433. 91	434. 132	435. 61	436. 96
437. 75	438. 156	439. 92	440. 103	441. 114	442. 65
443. 154	444. 100	445. 148	446. 36	447. 132	448. 120
449. 101	450. 137	451. 39	452. 96	453. 40	454. 40
455. 44	456. 81	457. 142	458. 118	459. 86	460. 153
461. 54	462. 116	463. 85	464. 138	465. 82	466. 128
467. 110	468. 78	469. 60	470. 148	471. 147	472. 129
473. 89	474. 134	475. 68	476. 145	477. 103	478. 47
479. 147	480. 75	481. 96	482. 85	483. 144	484. 65
485. 39	486. 103	487. 68	488. 160	489. 132	490. 105
491. 89	492. 24	493. 83	494. 135	495. 60	496. 106

Page 39: Subtraction: 1 through 100

497. 7	498. 68	499. 12	500. 32	501. 17	502. 21	503. 59
504. 33	505. 12	506. 19	507. 13	508. 49	509. 2	510. 21
511. 8	512. 5	513. 5	514. 5	515. 20	516. 4	517. 30
518. 16	519. 32	520. 60	521. 15	522. 25	523. 19	524. 18
525. 23	526. 27	527. 11	528. 30	529. 20	530. 30	531. 13
532. 6	533. 51	534. 4	535. 16	536. 19	537. 16	538. 53
539. 16	540. 7	541. 61	542. 4	543. 45	544. 0	545. 38
546. 53	547. 1	548. 40	549. 2	550. 3	551. 38	552. 22
553. 67	554. 18	555. 42	556. 2	557. 10	558. 64	559. 29
560. 77	561. 52	562. 15	563. 11	564. 57	565. 11	566. 43
567. 26	568. 11	569. 65	570. 10	571. 9	572. 9	573. 2
574. 12	575. 1	576. 18	577. 9	578. 9	579. 33	580. 44
581. 17	582. 5	583. 26	584. 25	585. 41	586. 9	587. 9
588. 3	589. 47	590. 9	591. 9	592. 21		

Page 45: Addition with Regrouping

593. 122	594. 113	595. 70	596. 112	597. 190	598. 112
599. 114	600. 33	601. 110	602. 110	603. 112	604. 130
605. 114	606. 146	607. 111	608. 160	609. 131	610. 111
611. 114	612. 110	613. 112	614. 145	615. 124	616. 111
617. 110	618. 121	619. 120	620. 134	621. 140	622. 172

623. 142	624. 110	625. 135	626. 145	627. 170	628. 21
629. 110	630. 131	631. 146	632. 122	633. 164	634. 12
635. 142	636. 110	637. 121	638. 173	639. 120	640. 150
641. 72	642. 66	643. 130	644. 144	645. 60	646. 120
647. 110	648. 30	649. 110	650. 190	651. 131	652. 20
653. 130	654. 140	655. 105	656. 122	657. 162	658. 110
659. 113	660. 120	661. 112	662. 115	663. 90	664. 110
665. 105	666. 121	667. 111	668. 154	669. 111	670. 86
671. 174	672. 144	673. 162	674. 152	675. 162	676. 160
677. 130	678. 127	679. 117	680. 160	681. 112	682. 123
683. 180	684. 170	685. 116	686. 133	687. 121	688. 160
689. 120	690. 123	691. 114	692. 150		

Page 50: Subtraction with Regrouping

693. 71	694. 3	695. 43	696. 13	697. 5	698. 19	699. 3
700. 52	701. 44	702. 18	703. 5	704. 6	705. 5	706. 11
707. 27	708. 5	709. 27	710. 37	711. 3	712. 8	713. 15
714. 5	715. 9	716. 33	717. 52	718. 6	719. 12	720. 47
721. 75	722. 16	723. 4	724. 12	725. 27	726. 32	727. 15
728. 42	729. 21	730. 49	731. 59	732. 67	733. 54	734. 31
735. 17	736. 0	737. 8	738. 48	739. 17	740. 16	741. 7
742. 29	743. 17	744. 23	745. 9	746. 1	747. 45	748. 25

749. 31   750. 3   751. 16   752. 8   753. 25   754. 37   755. 85

756. 46   757. 8   758. 69   759. 41   760. 24   761. 4   762. 1

763. 22   764. 7   765. 49   766. 7   767. 36   768. 51   769. 7

770. 11   771. 53   772. 2   773. 12   774. 47   775. 71   776. 26

777. 73   778. 43   779. 79   780. 43   781. 8   782. 18   783. 28

784. 22   785. 55   786. 27   787. 6   788. 13

Page 56: Make 100

789. 42   790. 32   791. 87   792. 27   793. 81   794. 26   795. 44

796. 3   797. 85   798. 55   799. 90   800. 97   801. 14   802. 75

803. 5   804. 1   805. 65   806. 69   807. 82   808. 12   809. 76

810. 25   811. 59   812. 13   813. 94   814. 30   815. 96   816. 6

817. 33   818. 51   819. 7   820. 9   821. 60   822. 93   823. 72

824. 88   825. 11   826. 84   827. 67   828. 46   829. 54   830. 77

831. 47   832. 83   833. 99   834. 29   835. 35   836. 63   837. 57

838. 68   839. 58   840. 24   841. 61   842. 34   843. 15   844. 78

845. 31   846. 28   847. 79   848. 20   849. 23   850. 95   851. 74

852. 49   853. 8   854. 17   855. 36   856. 45   857. 37   858. 40

859. 86   860. 22   861. 43   862. 38   863. 64   864. 91   865. 0

866. 41   867. 18   868. 10   869. 73   870. 39   871. 50   872. 89

873. 70   874. 21   875. 80   876. 71   877. 92   878. 66   879. 16

880. 62   881. 52   882. 98